ACTS OF THE APOSTLES

BOOKS BY CHARLES W. CONN

HISTORICAL
Like a Mighty Army
Where the Saints Have Trod
The Evangel Reader

DEVOTIONAL
The Rudder and the Rock
A Certain Journey

DOCTRINAL
Pillars of Pentecost

BIBLICAL
The Bible: Book of Books
A Guide to the Pentateuch
Christ and the Gospels
Acts of the Apostles

ACTS OF THE APOSTLES

CHARLES W. CONN

PATHWAY PRESS / CLEVELAND, TENNESSEE

Printed in the United States of America

I fondly
DEDICATE THIS BOOK
to my
friends and fellow laborers
across the nation
who have shared with me
in camp meetings and conferences
the glories of the Word of God,
with prayer that
the Lord Jesus Christ will be with us
as He was with the apostles
in the
BOOK OF ACTS

THE CHURCH TRAINING COURSE SERIES

Acts of the Apostles is written by Dr. Charles W. Conn and is one of the study books in the Bible course (CTC 206). A "Certificate of Credit" is awarded on the basis of the following requirements.

I. The book must be read through.

II. Training sessions must be attended unless permission for absence is granted by the instructor.

III. A written review must be completed and sent in to the state office. (No grade will be given for the written review.)

IV. The written review is not an examination but is designed to review the text. Students should research the text for the proper answers.

V. If no classes are conducted in this course of study, Church Training Course credit may be secured by home study.

A training record should be kept in the local church for each person who studies this and other courses in the Church Training Course program. A record form, CTC-33, will be furnished upon request from the state office. February and September are training months in the Church of God.

FOREWORD

A dynamic appeal for conservative, Bible-centered preaching and teaching has always characterized the ministry of Dr. Charles W. Conn. His latest book, *Acts of the Apostles,* continues this tradition. In this study text Dr. Conn makes a significant contribution to the layman's understanding of the Scriptures by presenting an enlightening review of the work of the young Christian church as it appears in Acts.

Presently the First Assistant General Overseer of the Church of God, Dr. Conn has served his church as pastor, editor, and church executive. As Editor in Chief of Church of God Publications and Editor of the *Evangel,* he gained wide respect for his sound weekly comment on the contemporary church scene. Publication of his denomination's church history, *Like a Mighty Army,* and a subsequent mission's history, *Where the Saints Have Trod,* established Conn as the foremost Pentecostal author of his day and gained him wide recognition as a leading church historian. His present position places him in the second highest administrative post in the Church of God. From this respected office he has again acquired great stature for his mature participation in guiding the growth of the church.

Acts of the Apostles, will add to the wealth of worthy writings that have flowed from the pen of Author Conn during the past two decades. It will likewise add to our understanding of one of the most significant books in the New Testament. Those who believe that the Bible is indeed divine revelation for man's redemption will find new truths in this study of God's company of the committed in the First Century.

Donald S. Aultman, director
National Sunday School and Youth Department

PREFACE

It has been said that every Christian should be engaged at all times in the serious study of some specific book of the Bible. Nothing adds more to Christian growth and development. I think it can be further said that every Christian should make a particular study of the Book of Acts. It is here that we see the problems of our own day in a first-century context. Most of the problems that we face, the apostles faced: they met the same opposition from the world; they were imperiled by false brethren and hypocrisy; they worked toward agreement among themselves; they faced the peril of popularity as well as the peril of persecution. In fact, the prototype of every present-day obstacle is seen in the experience of the apostles. In Acts we also observe the frailties of these men of God themselves. We see their weaknesses, their fears, their failures, as well as their forcefulness and their success.

Any book that sets forth such unending application to contemporary problems should be made the subject of determined study. It is hoped that every reader will make such a study of Acts. Primarily, this book is prepared as a guide for the Church Training Course program, but it is hoped that its usefulness will outlive this purpose. Every Christian should set upon a course of study in Acts that will continue until he has gained a thorough and workable understanding of one of the most fascinating books found in all sacred literature.

* * *

Writing this short guide has given me great pleasure and satisfaction. I hope that this will be observed by the reader in its pages. It has been inspiring to live again with the apostles whose deeds are recorded in the pages of Acts.

I hereby acknowledge and give thanks to those who have assisted in the preparation of the work.

Donald S. Aultman and Paul F. Henson have assisted greatly by their keen interest and pertinent suggestions.

Miss Carmen Holdman is especially appreciated for her capable preparation of the manuscript.

Mrs. Lucille Walker has been kind enough to read the manuscript and prepare it for the printers. Her suggestions and observations have been of great value.

And, as always, my wife has made even this modest task possible.

—*Charles W. Conn*

Cleveland, Tennessee
September 1, 1965

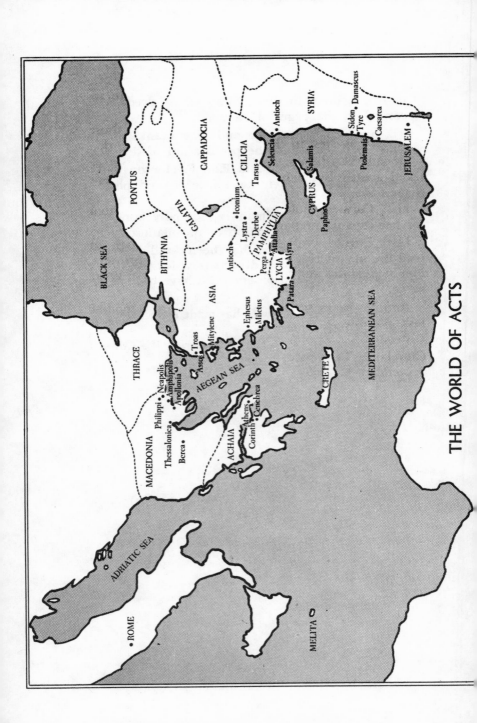

THE WORLD OF ACTS

Introduction to Acts

A BOOK FOR TODAY

More than any other book of the Bible, the Acts of the Apostles sets a pattern for our day. In terms of its practical application to the present time, it can be called the most important section of the Scriptures. All of the Bible is for us, and equally inspired, but Acts shows how the gospel of Jesus Christ was carried throughout the world in an age not greatly dissimilar to our own. With scant effort, the message, the methods, and many of the situations in Acts can be applied to our modern world and its problems.

Acts has a unique place in New Testament literature, for without it we would know practically nothing about what happened between the Gospels and the appearance of the Epistles. The period of history covered by Acts was a time of transition in which a simple Jewish faith, as the world supposed, swept across the world to the great city of Rome itself. The four Gospels record the life and ministry of Jesus, a relatively simple oral ministry, confined to Judea, a small province of the vast Roman Empire. The Epistles reveal a more advanced statement of doctrine in the form of learned letters written to Christian congregations in Asia Minor (Ga-

11

latia, Ephesus, and Colosse) and far away Europe
(Corinth, Philippi, Thessalonica, and Rome). The
transition from a Judean to a worldwide ministry
was a tremendous step. Except for a few incidental
hints in the epistolary literature, the Book of Acts
alone records how the transition came about.

In the Gospels we see Jesus as He laid the foundation of the gospel. Even when the disciples par-
ticipated in the labor, He was there to guide, direct,
or correct their efforts. The laying of the Christian
foundation occurred in Israel—and Jewish concepts,
customs, and background are everywhere apparent.
The Gospels, in brief, record the profound mystery
of the Incarnation and the profound simplicity of
Christ's teachings.

In the Epistles the body of Christian theology is
developed. These letters are formal statements of
Christian belief and behavior, presented in the main
to those who were already converted to Christian
faith.

Acts is the bridge between this foundation and
doctrinal development. It is the book that speaks
to our day in terms of action and achievement. It
is a record of what was done by men such as we are,
in a world much like our own. It is a glorious record.
In the Gospels we see a few unlearned Galilean
fishermen struggling to grasp the profound revelation of God. We see them unsure and uncertain of
their role in the Messianic revelation, often afraid,
timid, or discouraged. Yet, in Acts these men were
ready to take on the whole world for Jesus Christ.
These provincial Galileans become men to be reck-
oned with, men who shook their generation and
reshaped their world.

NAME OF THE BOOK

The book is commonly called *Acts of the Apostles,* but this is not a completely accurate designation. In many ways it is a misnomer. To begin with it does not really record the acts of the apostles. Of the original apostolic group, only three are mentioned. The death of James is recorded; John is seen briefly, though he never speaks; Peter is given more extensive treatment. But early in the history, even Peter passes from the scene. Thereafter the narrative follows the exploits of a convert to the faith—Saul (or Paul) of Tarsus in Asia Minor. In reality, Acts centers in the life of this enormous genius, who, though small man that he was, strode like a giant across the pages of history.

Many other names have been suggested as more appropriate to the book, such as *Gospel of the Holy Ghost, Acts of the Holy Spirit, Gospel of the Resurrection,* or *Acts of Apostolic Men.* In the earliest manuscripts no single title seemed to have general acceptance. Sometimes the book was simply designated as *The Acts,* or bore no title at all. Then came *Acts of Apostles,* and at last the present form was adopted—*The Acts of the Apostles.* One thing is very accurate about the title: the book is filled with action. It moves. It lives. On every page there is a vibrant pulsation of life and action.

We see Jesus living in His apostles, as the Vine bears its fruit through the branches. What Jesus began to do on earth He continues to do from His throne in heaven. The Holy Spirit, baptizing, filling, empowering, and guiding the apostles, acts boldly and purposefully through every page of the book.

THE AUTHOR

From the earliest days of the Church the Book of Acts has been regarded as the work of Luke. The author does not mention his name anywhere, but there are strong reasons for the Lukan view. First of all, Acts is inscribed to the same patron, Theophilus, as was the Gospel of Luke (Luke 1:3; Acts 1:1). The two books are clearly related by the writer's reference to "the former treatise." Also in light of their similar styles, the Third Gospel and the Book of Acts are obviously the works of the same author.

Furthermore, the author was not only intimate with the events recorded in the history, but he was also a participant in them. From chapter 16 onward the author frequently includes himself in the narrative. In three rather extended sections he employs the first person plural, which specifically places him in the midst of the action. Called the "we-sections," they are, Acts 16:10-17; 20:5—21:18; 27:1—28:16.

Luke was a constant and faithful companion of Paul, as is seen by numerous references to him in the Pauline Epistles. In Philemon 24, Luke is called a fellow laborer; in Colossians 4:14, he is called "the beloved physician"; and in 2 Timothy 4:11, he is mentioned as Paul's only companion as he awaited trial in a Roman prison.

While it is true that Paul had other loyal companions in the course of his ministry, practically all of these are mentioned in Acts in such a manner that they could not have been author of the book. The fact that Luke is not mentioned by name, and the fact that he definitely was with Paul combine to mark him as the careful historian of the sacred record.

But who was Luke? Little is known about him except for a few facts that can be deducted with a degree of certainty. He was a Gentile, very likely a Greek from Philippi. Not only was his name Greek, but his command of the Greek language was precise and expressive. He was able, both in the Third Gospel and in Acts, to exact from the Koine (the standard Greek) all its fluid, poetic beauty. He also wrote with the meticulous care for detail of a trained scientist; his background as a physician served him well even in his religious labors.

Of all the New Testament writers, Luke was the most painstaking and thorough. This characteristic also shows through in his faithfulness to the Christian gospel and its foremost herald, Paul. Even when others had fled as Paul awaited trial, Luke remained with him. He is a fortunate man who has a friend such as Luke; it is a fortunate cause that has a gifted advocate such as he.

WHY ACTS WAS WRITTEN

Luke was an excellent apologist. Under the inspiration of the Spirit, using careful research, and personally having "perfect understanding of all things from the very first" (Luke 1:3), Luke set forth the sure foundation of the Christian faith. In the strictest sense, Acts is not a history, for Luke made no attempt to give a comprehensive record of all the affairs of the Early Church. He makes no mention of Andrew, Matthew, Jude, Philip, Thomas, or other important apostles; he does not mention how James the Less rose to a position of authority in the Church; he does not refer to the evangelization of Egypt, or the Far Eastern lands, much of which took place early in the history of the Church.

He wrote as he was directed by the Holy Spirit. And what he wrote concerned the spread of the faith to Rome, by way of Palestine, Syria, Asia Minor, and Greece. The fact that Paul was in prison in Rome when Acts was written indicates that the record was needed there at that time. The book further-more records the manner in which the gospel was rejected by the Jews and received by the Gentiles. This was of great significance both then and now.

There is some opinion that the books of Luke and Acts were the first two volumes of a proposed three-volume history. If that were so, the third volume would probably have included the further ministry of Peter and Paul, and possibly others. While it could be tempting to speculate about what might have been included in such a further record, there is no reason to believe such a theory. It seems simply that the Holy Ghost concluded the inspired record at the appropriate point. Though more could have been written, there was no need for more. All that needed to be said had been said.

JESUS IN ACTS

The Book of Acts is merely a continuing record of the great supernatural event that began with the advent of Christ. In the Gospel of Luke we read of "all that Jesus began both to do and teach" (Acts 1:1). Underscore that word *began,* for it is the clue to our understanding of Acts. Just as the Gospel records what Jesus *began* to do, Acts records what He *continued* to do through His apostles. Our Lord's life on earth was but the beginning of His work and ministry. Through the agency of the Holy Spirit, and in the lives of His followers, He continued His mediatorial work of redemption and deliverance.

We see Jesus everywhere in Acts. He so constantly manifests Himself through the lives and deeds of His followers that miracles are as commonplace in Acts as they were in the Gospels. Jesus was not dead, but He lived on in those who served Him.

Jesus, as the already exalted king of Zion, appears, on all suitable occasions, as the ruler and judge of supreme resort; the apostles are but his representatives and instruments of working. It is He who appoints the twelfth witness, that takes the place of the fallen apostle; He who, having received the promise from the Father, sends down the Holy Spirit with power; He, who comes near to turn the people from their iniquities and add them to the membership of his church; He who works miracles from time to time by the hand of the apostles; who sends Peter to open the door of faith to the Gentiles; who instructs Philip to go and meet the Ethiopian; who arrests Saul in his career of persecution and makes him a chosen vessel to the Gentiles; in short, who continually appears presiding over the affairs of his church, directing his servants in their course, protecting them from the hands of their enemies, and in the midst of much that was adverse, still giving effect to their ministrations, and causing the truth of the gospel to grow and bear fruit.*

On the eve of His crucifixion the Lord said to His disciples:

I am the true vine, and my Father is the husbandman. Every branch in me that beareth not fruit he taketh away: and every branch that beareth fruit, he purgeth it, that it may bring forth more fruit. Now ye are clean through the

*Patrick Fairbairn, D.D., *Fairbairn's Imperial Standard Bible Encyclopedia.* (Grand Rapids, Michigan: Zondervan Publishing House, 1957), I, 95.

word which I have spoken unto you. Abide in me and I in
you. As the branch cannot bear fruit of itself, except it abide
in the vine; no more can ye, except ye abide in me. I am
the vine, ye are the branches. He that abideth in me, and
I in him, the same bringeth forth much fruit: for without
me ye can do nothing. If a man abide not in me, he is cast
forth as a branch, and is withered; and men gather them,
and cast them into the fire, and they are burned. If ye abide
in me, and my words abide in you, ye shall ask what ye
will, and it shall be done unto you. Herein is my Father
glorified, that ye bear much fruit; so shall ye be my disciples
(John 15:1-8).

In Acts we see the function of the branches as
they bear the fruit of the Vine. The Vine pours His
nature and energies through the branches and they
produce abundantly for Him. What He would do,
they do!

Also on His last night before the crucifixion, Jesus
said:

Nevertheless I tell you the truth; It is expedient for you
that I go away: for if I go not away, the Comforter will not
come unto you; but if I depart, I will send him unto you
(John 16:7).
I have yet many things to say unto you, but ye cannot
bear them now. Howbeit when he, the Spirit of truth, is
come, he will guide you into all truth: for he shall not speak
of himself; but whatsoever he shall hear, that shall he speak:
and he will shew you things to come. He shall glorify me:
for he shall receive of mine, and shall shew it unto you
(John 16:12-14).

In Acts we witness the Spirit as He guides the
apostles into the promised truth. Under the influence of the Spirit, those discouraged, unsure vessels
of clay become confident, courageous heralds of God.
There was no hindering or stopping the work of
Christ as it moved across the earth.

Acts opens with a final command to the disciples from their Lord before His ascension:

But ye shall receive power, after that the Holy Ghost is come upon you: and ye shall be witnesses unto me both in Jerusalem, and in all Judea, and in Samaria, and unto the uttermost part of the earth (Acts 1:8).

All the remainder of the book relates how the disciples fulfilled that charge. They carried the gospel first to Jerusalem; next, throughout Judea and Samaria; and at last to the world of their time. We shall observe more in this connection further on.

THE WORLD OF ACTS

The Book of Acts tells of the intrusion of the Christian message into a confused and evil time. It was a complex world that first heard the gospel of Christ, yet it was a world ripe for, and desperately in need of, that gospel.

The Roman Empire lay over all the known world. Its legions were stationed at outposts in even the remotest regions of the earth, its galleons plied the known seas, and its laws were rigidly applied toward the keeping of the peace. The communications and transportation systems of the empire were efficient and extensive. In many ways the exercise of empire was a blessing to the earth, but it was manifestly a mixed blessing. There were evils also, and these, like the law, were maintained by Rome's power of arms.

It was a day when half the world lay in the chains of dolorous slavery. Historian Gibbon estimates that the Roman Empire had a population of 120 million of which at least 60 million were slaves. It is for this reason that the gospel had so much to say about the suffering of man. In the Imperial City of Rome itself there were 900,000 slaves out of a population of 1,600,000. This means that more than half of the inhabitants of the proud city were slaves. Indeed, there were so many slaves that these unfortunate men were not allowed to wear any distinguishing dress, lest they become aware that they outnumbered their masters and rise up against them. The Roman power, for all its efforts to elevate the empire, thought little for the circumstance of the individual. Like a tyrant, the mightiest empire of ancient times held the world in its clutch.

It was a day when the common man believed in many strange gods, and the sophisticated man believed not at all. The temples of paganism had become places of riot and debauchery and there were few places for the contemplation of God.

It was a day of lust and orgy. Venus, Diana, and Aphrodite, goddesses of love, were served by priestess prostitutes, thousands strong in almost every major city, and their temples were sites of orgiastic revelry and promiscuity. Sexual license was so widespread that it left its mark even in the home, man's last sanctuary of decency. Seneca, a Roman philosopher of that time, commented on the breakdown of the home thus: "There are women who count their years . . . by the number of their husbands. Whoever has no love affairs is despised."

The day had become so evil, so far removed from God, that Scripture summarized the state of man in these descriptive words of Romans 1:21-31:

. . . When they knew God, they glorified him not as God, neither were thankful, but became vain in their imaginations,

and their foolish heart was darkened. Professing themselves
to be wise, they became fools, And changed the glory of the
uncorruptible God into an image made like to corruptible
man, and to birds, and four-footed beasts, and creeping things.
Wherefore God also gave them up to uncleanness through
the lusts of their own hearts, to dishonour their own bodies
between themselves: Who changed the truth of God into
a lie, and worshipped and served the creature more than
the Creator, who is blessed for ever. Amen. For this cause
God gave them up unto vile affections: for even their women
did change the natural use into that which is against nature:
And likewise also the men, leaving the natural use of the
woman, burned in their lust one toward another; men with
men working that which is unseemly, and receiving in themselves that recompence of their error which was meet. And
even as they did not like to retain God in their knowledge,
God gave them over to a reprobate mind, to do those things
which are not convenient; Being filled with all unrighteous-
ness, fornication, wickedness, covetousness, maliciousness; full
of envy, murder, debate, deceit, malignity, whisperers, Back-
biters, haters of God, despiteful, proud, boasters, inventors
of evil things, disobedient to parents, Without understanding,
covenant-breakers, without natural affection, implacable, un-
merciful.

And a mere handful of men actually tackled such
a world. Erstwhile timid and frightened, but now
emboldened by faith and empowered by the Holy
Spirit, they assailed the evil of their day. This situation is the point of Jesus' words:

> Behold, I send you forth as sheep in the midst of wolves:
> be ye therefore wise as serpents, and harmless as doves (Mat-
> thew 10:16).

Now one wolf in a flock of sheep is a marvel of
destruction and slaughter. Yet the circumstance of
the apostles was an infinitely greater peril than that—
they were lone sheep in the midst of a pack of wolves.

Only by leaning hard upon their Good Shepherd would they have a chance of survival and triumph.

But they did lean heavily upon Him. And everywhere in Acts we see Him present with them.

So the Book of Acts is the record of how a handful of men went forth in an evil day to spread the gospel of Christ. They not only labored in the shadow of the massive tree of Rome, but they followed the shadow to the very root of the tree itself. The record begins in Jerusalem and ends in Rome. It begins with only a few having any knowledge of Jesus Christ and ends with His name spread across many lands.

THE MESSAGE OF THE APOSTLES

These men had a message to proclaim to the world. That which had changed them from a band of craven cowards into a body of defiant challengers of the world could also happen in the lives of others. Theirs was a message of hope and courage, a message that transformed the lives of men. This message is summed up in these words:

So Paul, as he usually did, went to the synagogue, and for three sabbaths discussed with them the Scriptures, explaining them and proving that the Christ had to suffer and rise from the dead, and said, "This very Jesus whom I proclaim to you is the Christ" (Acts 17:2, 3, *Williams Translation*).

To the downcast, they could say: "Lift up your heads—Christ is alive!" To the weary they could say, "Come to Him and He will give you rest!" To the sick they could say, "Look to Him, for with His stripes you were healed!"

The message of Christ is a message of comfort and hope, for it is a message of victory and life.

The Resurrection had transformed the lives of the apostles, and as they proclaimed it, it transformed the lives of others. Christ had come "to preach the gospel to the poor . . . to heal the brokenhearted, to preach deliverance to the captives, and recovering of sight to the blind, to set at liberty those who were bruised, To preach the acceptable year of the Lord" (Luke 4:18, 19). His apostles carried on this great task.

So this was the message of the apostles. As they went, they preached; and as they preached, men heard; and as men heard, many believed; and as many as believed were filled with grace and glory and gladness of heart.

The message was to a world in sin and sorrow. Naturally it was heard most readily by the down-and-out, the toiler, the weary. But through them, by way of the servants' door, it in time entered the palace and was heard even by those who sat upon the throne.

The apostles preached and made converts with such zeal that by the time of their deaths they had won well over 500,000 souls to the living Christ. This was a miracle in itself; this was the glory of a Church that dared to believe and act upon that belief.

The apostles moved with boldness across the sin-blackened world and penetrated the darkness with blazing light. They turned a desperate time into a glorious age. By their preaching they made sinful men willing and happy to die for the Christ who offered forgiveness from sin and hope of resurrection unto life eternal.

DIVISION OF ACTS

There are numerous ways of outlining Acts. From early times some have seen it as a book of two sections:

The Acts of Peter (Chapters 1 through 12)
The Acts of Paul (Chapters 13 through 28)

Others have seen the book as containing two distinct stages:

The Jewish Age
The Gentile Age

Actually, however, the Book of Acts provides its own natural divisions, set forth by Jesus just before His ascension:

But ye shall receive power, after that the Holy Ghost is come upon you: and ye shall be witnesses unto me both
in Jerusalem,
and in all Judea,
and in Samaria,
and unto the uttermost part of the earth (Acts 1:8).

This is precisely what happened. The apostles began their witness in Jerusalem then spread outward into all of Judea. The message was next carried into Samaria, which was essentially a phase of the Jewish ministry. Then the Good News was carried into the Gentile world—across Asia Minor, into Greece, and on into Italy.

Thus the drama of Acts opens in the Holy City, Jerusalem, and closes in the Imperial City, Rome.

OUTLINE OF ACTS OF THE APOSTLES

I. THE FOUNDATION IS LAID (1:1-26)
   A. *The Prologue* (1:1, 2)
   B. *Jesus' Promise of the Spirit* (1:3-8)
   C. *The Ascension of Jesus* (1:9-11)
   D. *The Disciples Wait for the Spirit* (1:12-14)
   E. *The Selection of Matthias* (1:15-26)

II. WITNESS TO JERUSALEM (2:1—7:60)
   A. *The Day of Pentecost* (2:1-41)
      1. The Holy Spirit Comes (2:1-4)
      2. The First Witnesses (2:5-13)
      3. The First Sermon (2:14-40)
      4. The First Converts (2:41)
   B. *The Church Begins* (2:42-47)
   C. *The Ministry of Peter and John* (3:1—4:31)
      1. A Lame Man Is Healed (3:1-26)
      2. Persecution Comes (4:1-22)
      3. Refilling of the Spirit (4:23-31)
   D. *Growth and Trouble in Jerusalem* (4:32—6:7)
      1. The Sharing of Possessions (4:32-37)
      2. The Sin of Ananias and Sapphira (5:1-11)
      3. Peter's Shadow Heals the Sick (5:12-16)
      4. Persecution Increases (5:17-42)
      5. Seven Assistants Are Chosen (6:1-7)
   E. *The Witness and Death of Stephen* (6:8—7:60)

III. WITNESS TO JUDEA AND SAMARIA (8:1—12:25)
   A. *The Disciples Are Scattered* (8:1-4)
   B. *Philip's Ministry in Samaria* (8:5-40)
      1. Miracles of Philip (8:5-8)
      2. Simon the Sorcerer (8:9-25)
      3. The Ethiopian Eunuch (8:26-40)

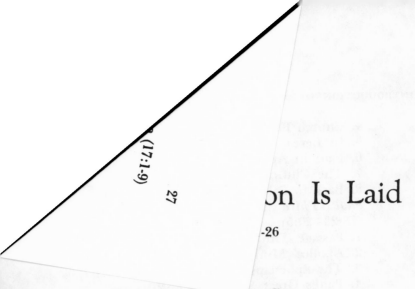

A. THE PROLOGUE (1:1, 2)

It must be borne in mind that Acts is the second
volume of a two-part work. The *Gospel of Luke*
and the *Acts of the Apostles* were written as one
extensive record of the Christian movement. Luke
inscribed both volumes to someone called Theophilus. The name itself comes from two Greek words—
theos, which means "God," and *philein,* which means
"to love." Literally, the name meant "Friend of
God." It was a custom of those days for an author
to address a published work to the patron who sponsored it. It was also customary to inscribe a work
to some notable person out of a sense of appreciation.
When, in Luke 1:3, Theophilus was called "most
excellent," we get the impression that he was someone of governmental rank and prestige. In the *Knox
Translation* he is called "most noble Theophilus."
Possibly he was an official of Rome who needed
or desired to know about the background of the
Christian movement. Another possibility is that Theophilus was a person of wealth who had sponsored
Luke's education. It was customary for one whose

training had been provided by another to dedicate
a portion of his future labors to that patron.

Some believe that Theophilus referred to no particular person but was merely a name used to desig-
nate all those who were followers of God. Though
no one will likely ever know, it seems reasonable
that he was a Greek nobleman or Roman official
who was interested in Christianity and sought an
authentic and authoritative record of it.

B. PROMISE OF THE SPIRIT (1:3-8)

There is a strong natural overlap between the
closing section of Luke (24:46-53) and the opening
section of Acts (1:1-14). Because Acts is a sequel to
Luke, this overlap is the bridge that joins the two
parts together. More than that, both sections underscore the cardinal factors of the Christian faith and
the ministry of the Church. They contain:

- An emphasis on the Lord's resurrection.
- The promise of the Holy Spirit and the power
  of His infilling.
- The record of the disciples' tarrying in Jeru-
  salem for the Holy Spirit.
- The commission to bear witness to Christ in
  all the world, beginning in Jerusalem.
- The account of the Lord's ascension.

The end of Jesus' work on earth was only the
beginning of what He was to do. He would do His
greatest work through His followers. The Gospel of
Luke recorded what He began to do and teach (Acts
1:1), while Acts recorded what He continued to do.

The fact of the Resurrection was the foundation of the disciples' faith, and this was essential to the continuing ministry of Christ. Knowledge that He was Master over death and evermore alive transformed these men and sent them forth as heralds of hope. For this reason Jesus revealed Himself to His followers many times during the forty days between His resurrection and ascension. Luke called these appearances "infallible proofs" (1:3). They so thoroughly confirmed the deity of Christ that there is not the slightest indication of later doubt in any of those who beheld Him.

In similar manner, the ascension of Jesus confirmed His Lordship. This event was far more than the mere consummation of His life on earth. It was the return to His pre-incarnate glory. It was His return to the right hand of the Father, where He would participate directly and positively in the sovereign rule of God. This was fulfillment of the supreme lordship of Christ. (See Acts 7:56; 1 Corinthians 15:24-28; Romans 8:34; Philippians 2:9-11; Ephesians 2:20-23.) The Ascension was the completion of the Resurrection, as the Resurrection was the completion of the Crucifixion.

Directly related to the ascension was Jesus' promise of the Holy Spirit (John 16:7). Several times on the evening before His crucifixion Jesus emphasized that the Holy Spirit would come to the disciples after His departure from them (John 14:16, 17, 26; 15:26; 16:7-17). The effusion of the Holy Ghost would be the apostles' enablement to carry on the work of Jesus. In the marvelous manner in which all the things of God interlock and intertwine, only the power of the Holy Spirit made the apostles effective witnesses for the Lord. The commission to witness was founded upon the promise of the Spirit (Acts 1:8).

C. THE ASCENSION OF JESUS (1:9-11)

The departure of Jesus from the earth was as majestic and triumphant as His coming had been. Having completed His admonition concerning the Holy Ghost, Jesus was taken up into the sky and enveloped in a cloud which hid Him from the view of His awestruck disciples.

That which received Jesus was no ordinary cloud, but the *Shekinah* which was so often associated with the presence of God. (See Exodus 13:21; Exodus 40:34; 1 Kings 8:10; 1 Corinthians 10:1, 2; Matthew 24:30; Revelation 1:7.) This heavenly cloud covered the Lord of Heaven as He returned to His eternal, celestial domain.

It is easy to imagine what emotions the disciples felt as they beheld His ascension. There was certainly awe, with a touch of sadness at the thought that Jesus was gone from them, and at least a swell of joy in their hearts. Two men, angels of the Lord, appeared to the disciples and gave them the promise that:

This same Jesus, which is taken up from you into heaven, shall so come in like manner as ye have seen him go into heaven (Acts 1:11).

The ascension of Jesus was of twofold significance. First of all, it signified the reality of heaven and the fact that Jesus and His mission are heavenly. We see heaven no matter how we look at this glorious event. It puts the unfading stamp of heaven upon

all subsequent work for Jesus. Ours is no mere earthly life, for all that we are and do in Him comes
from, and returns to, heaven.

Second, the ascension of Jesus gave testimony to
His second coming. As surely as He went away, He
shall "in like manner" return to the earth. Everything about His departure from the earth affirms
that He shall return "in the clouds of heaven with
power and great glory" (Matthew 24:30).

D. THE DISCIPLES WAIT FOR THE SPIRIT (1:12-14)

It was in an attitude of worship that the disciples
returned to Jerusalem from the Mount of Olives.
According to Luke 24:53, they spent much time in
the Temple worshiping God, and Acts tells us that
they "abode" in an upper room. In all likelihood,
and according to universal beliefs, the upper room
was that same room where Jesus had observed the
Passover with His disciples. This would have been
the logical place for His followers to wait for the
Holy Spirit to come. The proper understanding
seems to be that the disciples alternated between
the Temple and the upper room.

Besides the apostles, there were numerous women
among those who worshiped and waited. From the
beginning of His ministry Jesus had been mindful
of the sincere worship and service of women. In
Luke 8:2, 3 we have a list of some who accompanied
the throng on the Lord's preaching missions, such
women as Mary Magdalene, Joanna, Susanna, "and
many others." In a region and time where women
were of generally low estate, Jesus lifted them to

a status of dignity and made them equal with man in worship and service. The list of women we find in the story of His earthly life is impressive.

Mary, the mother of Jesus, was present in the upper room. The fact that Joseph was not mentioned indicates that he was no longer alive. The brothers of Jesus were also present. These are named in Mark 6:3 as James, Joses, Simon, and Judah. They would all have been younger than Jesus. These brethren had previously doubted and misunderstood Jesus (John 7:5), but they apparently became convinced of His divinity. During the forty days after His resurrection the Lord appeared to James (1 Corinthians 15:7), who, though obscure in Jesus' lifetime, rose to prominence in the Early Church.

The chief occupation of this waiting group was prayer. It is probable that they attended the set hours of prayer in the Temple (see Luke 24:53 and Acts 2:46), for they had been trained to pray in this way. But there was a new content in their praying. Jesus had spoken of the promise of the Father; and for the fulfillment of that promise, for the baptism with the Holy Spirit, they prayed continually. Until the promise came, they could only wait.*

E. THE SELECTION OF MATTHIAS (1:15-26)

During the course of their praying and tarrying for the Holy Spirit, the disciples took time to care for one urgent matter. The circle of twelve apostles had been reduced to eleven by the terrible sin of Judas. It was Peter who took the lead in this matter, for already he was assuming the leadership which

---

*Albert C. Winn, *The Acts of the Apostles* (*The Layman's Bible Commentary*, Vol. XX, edited by Balmer H. Kelley. Richmond, Virginia: John Knox Press, 1960), p. 24.

had been foreseen during the Lord's life. Peter reviewed the downfall of Judas, related the tragic manner of his death, then explained the need of choosing
a replacement for the traitor.

This is an important section for it gives the function and qualifications of an apostle. An apostle
must be one who had been with Jesus throughout
the course of His ministry. He must be a continuing
witness to the resurrection of Jesus. There would
be other apostles—such as Barnabas and Paul—but
to be one of the Twelve, one must have had the
background of constant companionship with Jesus.

The Jewish method of making choices was the
casting of lots. So this method was followed by the
first Christians. It was a mixture of human voting
and providential selection. The casting of lots has
been described in this way:

> It may seem to us strange that the method was that of
> casting lots. But amongst the Jews it was the natural thing
> to do, because all the offices and duties in the Temple were
> settled by lot. The normal way of doing it was that the
> names of the candidates were written on stones; the stones
> were then put into a vessel and the vessel was shaken until
> one stone fell out; and he whose name was on the first stone
> to fall out was elected to office.*

The disciples chose Joseph Barsabas and Matthias,
both of whom met the qualifications of an apostle.
They prayed for God to make the final selection,
then they cast lots. Matthias was chosen. We know
nothing of Matthias, either of his previous history
or his later life. We can only assume that he was

_____
*William Barclay, *The Acts of the Apostles* (Daily Study Bible Series,
Philadelphia: The Westminster Press, 1955), p. 10.

a person of admirable qualities to have the confidence of the disciples and the selection of the lot.

With this we come to the end of all preparatory matters. The foundation for apostolic witness was laid, solid and secure, and the faithful ones now only waited for the promise of the Spirit.

Witness to Jerusalem

Acts 2:1—7:60

A. THE DAY OF PENTECOST (2:1-4)

1. The Holy Spirit Comes (2:1-4). The feast of
Pentecost was one of the three most important fes-
tivals of Israel. It commemorated both the giving
of the Law on Mt. Sinai and the firstfruits of the
harvest. The word *Pentecost* means "the fiftieth day"
and was given to the festival because it fell on the
fiftieth day after the Passover.

Because of its significance and the time of its observance (the latter part of May or the first part of
June) many Jews thronged to Jerusalem for the
observance of Pentecost. It is said that more came
to the Holy City for Pentecost than were there for
the Passover. Certainly there were as many. The
listing found in Acts 2:5, 9-11 indicates from what
distant places the dispersed Jews poured back into
their homeland.

The week preceding the Day of Pentecost was
filled with various observances, all in preparation
for the day itself. The day itself brought the festival
to a high peak of worship and celebration. Through
the years, however, the solemn day had become less

than spiritual through numerous excesses that had intruded the occasion. As it was rather commonplace for the celebrants to become drunk, this was thought to be the case of those who were filled with the Holy Ghost.

On the Day of Pentecost, as the festive celebration reached its peak, the spiritual worship reached its peak in the upper room. There the 120 disciples of Jesus were gathered "with one accord"—that is, they all had a single purpose. Their prayer, their desire, their determination had reached a rare point of unity. This expression of unity is prominent throughout the Book of Acts (1:14; 2:1; 4:32; 5:12). Though the little band of 120 in the upper room were unnoticed amid the teeming multitude of pilgrims in Jerusalem, they had reached a place of spiritual receptivity beyond the comprehension of merely religious men. They were vessels ready to be filled.

Suddenly, marvelously, the disciples were filled with the Holy Ghost. Just as Jesus promised, the Spirit came to them. The infilling of the Holy Spirit was accompanied by three unusual phenomena: the house was filled with a rushing wind-like sound; forked tongues like flames of fire appeared above and settled upon the heads of each of the 120; and all of them began speaking in tongues, or languages they did not understand.

It was an occasion of unequaled importance in the history of the Christian faith. What happened in the upper room was the most significant event of the Apostolic age, or of any subsequent age. The coming of the Holy Spirit is clearly the most important single event the Church has ever seen. Without it there would have been no Church. It was the

final act of Christ's revelation of God. And it was
the effusion that enabled the disciples to perpetuate
His message.

Without the Day of Pentecost the movement
Christ began would have slowly sunk back into the
body of Judaism. The name of Jesus would be re-
membered as a pious, wise prophet whom God used
marvelously, but he would not be known as the In-
carnate God. Only the coming of the Spirit could
do that. Jesus Himself had said:

And I will pray the Father, and he shall give you another
Comforter, that he may abide with you for ever; Even the
Spirit of truth; whom the world cannot receive, because it
seeth him not, neither knoweth him: but ye know him; for
he dwelleth with you, and shall be in you. I will not leave
you comfortless: I will come to you. Yet a little while, and
the world seeth me no more; but ye see me: because I live,
ye shall live also. At that day we shall know that I am in
my Father, and ye in me, and I in you (John 14:16-20).

It was the coming of the Holy Spirit that eternally
demonstrated Christ's oneness with the Father, and
His spiritual union with His followers. It was, furthermore, the Spirit who was to bring the ultimate
glory to Christ:

Nevertheless I tell you the truth; It is expedient for you
that I go away: for if I go not away, the Comforter will not
come unto you; but if I depart, I will send him unto you.
And when he is come, he will reprove the world of sin, and
of righteousness, and of judgment: Of sin, because they
believe not on me; Of righteousness, because I go to my
Father, and ye see me no more; Of judgment, because the
prince of this world is judged. I have yet many things to
say unto you, but ye cannot bear them now. Howbeit when
he, the Spirit of truth, is come, he will guide you into all
truth: for he shall not speak of himself; but whatsoever he

shall hear, that shall he speak: and he will shew you things to come. He shall glorify me: for he shall receive of mine, and shall shew it unto you (John 16:7-14).

Moreover, the Spirit was to testify of Christ and empower the disciples to do the same:

But when the Comforter is come, whom I will send unto you from the Father, even the Spirit of truth, which proceedeth from the Father, he shall testify of me: And ye also shall bear witness, because ye have been with me from the beginning (John 15:26, 27).

It was the coming of the Holy Spirit that made it possible for this band of devout followers of Christ to become an unconquerable body of witnesses to Him. On the Day of Pentecost this small Jewish band was forged into the Church of God.

2. *The First Witnesses (2:5-13).* The witness of the disciples began immediately. Jews and proselytes from fifteen sections of the world are mentioned as being in Jerusalem on the Day of Pentecost: from Parthia, Media, Elam, Mesopotamia, Judea, Cappadocia, Pontus, Asia, Phrygia, Pamphylia, Egypt, Cyrene, Rome, Crete, and Arabia! This was not necessarily an exhaustive listing of those nations represented, but it gives an idea of the universal nature of the occasion. The marvelous point is that all these lingual groups heard the Spirit-filled disciples speaking their languages. This was the initial witness of the Risen Christ to a bewildered world.

The experience was of an ecstatic nature. This is seen by the assumption of the people that the disciples were drunk. Of the three phenomena, however, the multitude witnessed only one—the speaking in tongues. The rushing wind and the tongues of fire were heard and seen only by the disciples—and these never recurred in later outpourings of the Holy Spirit. Although the speaking in tongues was frequently manifested, the other signs seem to have been particularly for this initial outpouring, and even then only for the disciples to hear and see.

3. *The First Sermon (2:14-36)*. Peter, seeing the confused and doubtful throng of Jews, seized the opportunity to preach the gospel. He and the other apostles had preached earlier when Jesus sent them out (Luke 9:1, 2), but this was the first effort since His death and resurrection. It was the first specifically Christian sermon, and the first recorded sermon of an apostle.

The courage required of Peter to preach his message would be difficult to overestimate. Only recently the mob had demanded the death of Jesus, and they were not above doing the same to Peter. Only recently Peter had been intimidated by the taunts of a wanton girl. Now he stood before the explosive throng and preached. All the apostles stood with him, signifying that what he had to say was being said by them all. Peter was merely the spokesman for the entire company.

In his long sermon, only a portion of which is recorded (2:40), Peter began by explaining the outpouring of the Spirit. After all, this is what had drawn the crowd together. He explained that the disciples' behavior was caused not by drunkenness, but was the fulfillment of prophecy. Peter quoted Joel 2:28-32 to explain the events of the day.

Then Peter reviewed the life of Jesus and gave eloquent testimony to Him. It is a simple yet pro-

found declaration that Jesus was the Christ—He was
Saviour and Lord. The apostle did not hesitate to
charge the Jews with the death of Jesus. Nevertheless, he declared, the Crucifixion was according to
the predeterminate counsel of God the Father. The
Jews in their act of malice had ironically given proof
to the divinity of Jesus and the redemptive plan of
God.

This was a strong, bold sermon. It required great
insight into the cause and consequence of a tragedy
that had happened only fifty days earlier. This early
perceptivity can be explained only by the inspiration
of the Holy Spirit.

4. The First Converts (2:37-41). The effect of
Peter's sermon was electric. Many of those who listened to him were among those who only recently
had cried "Crucify Him!" Upon hearing their of-
fence spelled out to them with such urgent eloquence, they showed evidence of a quickened sense
of guilt.

"Men and brethren," they cried, "what shall we
do?"

Their guilt went deeper, however, than the single
act of crucifixion. They stood as sinners in need of
conversion to a new life in Christ. If they would now
repent and be baptized in the name of Jesus Christ
so that their sins might be forgiven, they would
be able to partake of the great outpouring of the
Holy Spirit.

A large number responded to the appeal. About
3,000 were won to Christ and baptized that very day.

How wonderful are the ways of God's grace! Many
of those who only fifty days earlier had been de-

manding the crucifixion of Jesus now accepted Him
as Saviour and Lord. They were now redeemed from
sin by the very blood they so recently had demanded
to be shed. They were made partakers of that life
they had so recently endeavored to extinguish.

B. THE CHURCH BEGINS (2:42-47)

Immediately the branches began to bear fruit of
the Vine. Though the Christians continued to observe the Jewish worship, such as regular prayer in
the Temple, they performed miracles and signs un-
like any work seen in the Temple. Such activities
filled the people of the Holy City with awe and
wonder.

From the outset, the Christians were drawn together in a strong bond of fellowship. They even
shared their meals together. Two reasons would account for their closeness. For, they naturally had
a deep sense of unity and affinity. Theirs was a spiritual unity and singleness of purpose. Even today
those who are in Christ enjoy and appreciate one
another, for fellowship is both a proof and a blessing
of the Christian life.

Secondly, danger served to draw them together.
It was dangerous for a man to proclaim faith in
Jesus in those days. Abetted by their religious leaders,
many Jews maintained that Jesus was a religious
blasphemer, a rebel, a threat to the Jewish faith and
people. Harassment and persecution were very real
and could, on occasion, explode into violence. It
was therefore safer for the Christians to stay together,
and needful for strength and encouragement.

Not only did the Christians band themselves together, but they sold their property and pooled their assets into a community treasury. From this common fund they provided for each person's needs.

As the church in Jerusalem grew rapidly in numbers, it also grew strong in love and fellowship. The Christians were an irrepressibly happy group. Neither persecution nor difficulty daunted their joy in the Lord. Note the characteristics of this church as indicated in verses 42, 45, and 46:

> Doctrine
> Fellowship
> Breaking of bread
> Prayer
> Signs and wonders
> Unity
> Liberality
> Gladness
> Singleness of heart

With these characteristics the church of today can have the success and effectiveness of that apostolic band.

C. THE MINISTRY OF PETER AND JOHN (3:1—4:31)

1. A Lame Man Is Healed (3:1-26). Just as they had been prominent among the Lord's disciples while He was alive, Peter and John were the conspicuous leaders of the Early Church. Luke records one incident that serves to illustrate the way in which these two men bore witness to Christ in Jerusalem.

At first the disciples had no thought of withdrawing from the fold of historic Judaism. They were simple Jews who believed that Jesus was the long-awaited Messiah. Their task, as they understood it, was to convince their fellow Jews of this fact. Accordingly, they followed all the customary practices of worship, including prayer in the Temple three times a day—the third, sixth, and ninth hours after sunrise: at 9 a.m., 12 noon, and 3 p.m.

It was during the mid-afternoon that Peter and John encountered a lame man sitting, as was customary in the East, at the gate of the Temple, begging the worshipers for money. Peter and John accepted his solicitation as an opportunity to witness for Christ. In His name the two disciples healed the man.

The effect of the healing was immediate: the man began "walking and leaping and praising God." This ecstatic action from the healed man drew a throng of curious spectators, and once again Peter seized the opportunity to preach the gospel. It is interesting that it was so often Peter who spoke out for the Christian group:

And in those days Peter stood up in the midst of the disciples, and said . . . (1:15).
But Peter, standing up with the eleven, lifted up his voice, and said unto them . . . (2:14).
Then Peter said unto them . . . (2:38).
And when Peter saw it, he answered unto the people . . . (3:12).
Then Peter, *filled with the Holy Ghost,* said unto them . . . (4:8).

The bold, outspoken apostle was by now "the Rock," able to strengthen and support his brethren as Jesus had instructed him (Luke 22:32). The potential qualities Jesus had seen in Peter were at last realized.

The sermon of Peter on this occasion closely followed that of the Day of Pentecost. Once again he referred to the fact that Jesus was the fulfillment of the Jewish expectation. The Jewish people had rejected and killed Him—"the Prince of life, whom God hath raised from the dead; whereof we are witnesses (3:15)."

But God would forgive them. Not only were they guilty of the death of Christ, but they were in need of redemption from sin. Christ came to turn men from iniquity:

It was to you first that God sent his servant after he had raised him up to bring you great blessing by turning every one of you away from his evil ways (3:26, *Phillips Translation*.)*

2. Persecution Comes (4:1-22). If the sermon was similar to that of the Day of Pentecost, the results were different. The Sadducees acted in violent reflex to the message of the Resurrection, which they held to be blasphemy. They were so stung by the rapid growth of the new doctrine that they arrested the two apostles. Because it was too late for a hearing that day, the apostles were kept in custody until the next day. Despite this, "many of them which heard the word believed" (4:4), and the Church increased to a total of about five thousand men.

Peter and John were tried before the same Sanhedrin that had tried Jesus. On that fateful night when Jesus was tried, John had gone into the courtroom, but Peter had stood back, timid and afraid. Now both men were bold as lions. There was no

---

*From *The New Testament in Modern English, Copyright* J. B. Phillips, 1958. Used by permission of The Macmillan Company.

flinching, no recoiling. With Spirit-filled audacity Peter confronted the Sanhedrin, the highest court in Israel, and charged them with crucifying Jesus. He declared that they were not only guilty of killing Jesus, but also that they could never be saved until they reversed their position to the point of actually believing on Him:

Neither is there salvation in any other: for there is none other name under heaven given among men, whereby we must be saved (Acts 4:12).

Dumbfounded by the boldness of Peter and John, and conscious of the undeniable healing the apostles had performed, the court sought a quiet solution. Because of the general favor the miracle had gained in the city, the court was afraid to punish Peter and John. Since they could not deny the miracle, they sought to suppress it. So they commanded them not to preach or teach any more in the name of Jesus.

But Peter and John rejected the command, though they were aware of what the consequences might be. They made it known that they would obey God rather than man—and God had ordained them to preach.

Finally, "because of the people: for all men glorified God for that which was done," with nothing but further threats, made in an effort to cover their confusion, the Sanhedrin let the bold apostles go.

3. *Refilling of the Spirit (4:23-31)*. The experience of Peter and John did not discourage the disciples or hinder their devotion. Instead, it precipitated a time of joyous worship. Once again, even in their prayers, we find the expression "with one accord." This indicates the nature of their united prayers,

for in all likelihood they prayed in unison, with concerted praise.

The prayer of the disciples, as recorded by Luke, is one of the most beautiful portions of the New Testament. It has a lofty psalm-like quality. The prayer was predominantly an expression of praise, with very little petition. And the petition it does contain is only for boldness that the disciples might even more fearlessly proclaim the gospel. They ask for more spiritual power so that more healings, more signs and wonders, might be performed for the glory of Jesus Christ. In this, prayer reached a noble and spiritual height unknown to men who only pray for things.

The prayer was answered by a new filling of the Holy Ghost. This does not imply that there was a depletion of the Spirit following the initial outpouring on Pentecost. This was a new manifestation of power, an enlargement of spiritual capacity and fullness.

Just as the initial outpouring had given the Christians irrefutable courage, the new anointing gave them even increased boldness. This boldness was a direct result of the Holy Spirit in their lives. This is good, for any other form of bravery would have been either recklessness or ignorance. But they were courageous for a cause; they had a purpose beyond themselves. This is the boldness needed today—the responsible boldness and the enduring fortitude that the Holy Spirit gives.

D. GROWTH AND TROUBLE IN JERUSALEM (4:32—6:7)

1. *The Sharing of Possessions (4:32-37).* The com-

munal sharing of goods that had been started earlier
(2:44) was soon applied to an advanced degree. Spon-
taneously and voluntarily the disciples sold their
houses and lands and pooled their resources.

Why?

Perhaps it was because they felt that the Lord
would soon return and they would thereafter have
no need of houses and lands. Perhaps it was because
the disciples already comprehended that Jerusalem
would soon be destroyed and merely divested themselves of the property they knew was to be lost. Perhaps it was because the equal sharing of wealth was
under the circumstances a beautiful Christian ideal.

This sincere demonstration of brotherly love was
evidently started by Barnabas, a well-to-do disciple
from Cyprus. It was clearly a gesture of generosity,
but it has led to much discussion ever since. Some
claim that this was the divine way. Others have called
it communistic, for the practice indeed followed such
a principle.

There are several things that should be observed.
First, the practice was started without any directive
from God to do so. This does not mean that it was
wrong, only that it was not commanded. The Christians seem to have acted according to what seemed
best to them.

Observe next, that only the Christians in Jerusalem followed the practice. As the faith spread there
is no suggestion that the Christians in Antioch, Damascus, or other places disposed of their individual
property and lived from a common treasury. It was
apparently confined to the church in Jerusalem.

Then, you will notice, the experiment did not
work. From the outset it gave rise to problems that

affected the very fellowship that gave birth to the idea. Two of the group succumbed to the temptation of covetousness and attempted fraud in the matter (5:1-10). Quarreling and disputings arose when some felt that they were not receiving their fair share (6:1). Finally, the experiment may have helped produce an impoverished church. It is possible that this is one reason the Christians in Antioch had to send famine relief to the Christians in Jerusalem (11:27). When the time of famine came and the treasury of the church was exhausted, the disciples were without further means.

The pooling of material goods might have been a beautiful idea—if all other factors had been ideal. But they were not. The plan did not work.

The principle of sharing and assistance does work, and is even today one of the prominent features of the Christian experience. Though Christ never demanded the pooling of assets, He does demand the assisting of those in need (James 2:15, 16; 1 John 3:17, 18).

2. The Sin of Ananias and Sapphira (5:1-11). The death of Ananias and Sapphira is one of the most widely discussed, yet little understood, incidents of the New Testament. This man and wife pretended to sacrifice their possessions without actually doing so. They wanted credit without performance and recognition without worthiness.

It must be observed that Ananias and Sapphira were under no requirement to sell their possessions and give the proceeds to the church, yet when they pretended to do so they set an example of deceit in the church. They "lied to God." The judgment

of God was swift and direct. First Ananias fell dead.
He was hastily buried in order to get his body out
of the community. Upon hearing of her husband's
death, Sapphira also fell dead.

This was severe judgment. Many have felt that
it was too severe. But we must bear in mind that
God was dealing with a matter that would have
quickly corrupted the entire Christian cause. His
swift penalty for lying to the Holy Ghost brought
a wholesome fear to the whole church. Twice this is
observed: "great fear came on all them that heard
these things" (v. 5), and "great fear came upon the
church, and upon as many as heard these things"
(v. 11).

It is healthy to learn that we are not to trifle with
sacred things. "The fear of the Lord is the beginning
of knowledge" (Proverbs 1:7).

3. Peter's Shadow Heals the Sick (5:12-16). As the
Christians continued their witness in Jerusalem, the
example of Ananias and Sapphira had a solemn effect on the church. The disciples already knew that
they faced danger from the outside when they claimed
faith in Christ; now they knew that they also faced
danger on the inside if they claimed a greater piety
than they really possessed. In such a strait as this
one either has a profound dedication to Christ or
one does not stand at all.

Nothing cures a church of trifling and tempers
it for service more quickly than the presence of persecution on the outside and the threat of judgment
on the inside. The disciples increased marvelously
under such pressure. "Believers were the more added
to the Lord, multitudes both of men and women."

Peter was held in such respect that even his shadow effected healing as he walked past those who were sick and afflicted. Now we know that it is impossible for virtue to be in a shadow, for a shadow is only the absence of light. It has no substance whatever; yet Peter's shadow effected healing. This was a dramatic example of what faith the great apostle inspired. The people so honored him, and the Christ he served, that they were healed when he even passed between them and the sun.

It was at this point that the witness of the Church began to reach beyond the borders of Jerusalem. The people came to the Christians from the environs of the Holy City and other cities nearby. Just as Jesus healed all who came to Him, so the apostles healed all who came to them.

4. Persecution Increases (5:17-42). Although the Sadducees were for a time reluctant to arrest the apostles again, they could stand the success of the Church no longer. Filled with jealousy, they finally did arrest and imprison them. But God delivered the apostles from prison by sending an angel to open the prison doors. They were not told to flee, but to continue their witness of the new life.

When the Sanhedrin Council met the following day they found the apostles in the Temple teaching the people. It was as if some great joke had been played on the authorities. The high priest paid the apostles a high compliment by saying "Ye have filled Jerusalem with your doctrine."

The council became eager to clear themselves of blame in the death of Jesus. Only recently they had said through the irresponsible multitude, "His blood

be on us, and on our children" (Matthew 27:20, 25;
John 19:6). Now they were concerned lest His blood
be brought upon them (5:28). They tried to disclaim
any responsibility in the death of Jesus.

Peter, however, once again placed the blame of
Jesus' crucifixion squarely on the council. Moreover,
he again refused to quit preaching the doctrine of
Christ. Cut and stung, the authorities began a con-
spiracy to put the apostles to death. Except for the
wise counsel of Gamaliel, a Pharisee, the Sadducees
might have achieved their purpose. This man—one
of Israel's great teachers, instructor of Saul of Tarsus,
and grandson of the great Hillel—was a respected
and sage authority of the Law. He recommended
patience and care, lest the Sanhedrin find itself in
conflict with God. It is not likely that Gamaliel
believed the teaching of the apostles, for there is no
indication of his ever accepting Christ. He was merely a wise and prudent teacher, a profound believer
in the sovereign will of God.

The wisdom of Gamaliel prevailed. The apostles
were not killed, but only beaten. What the nature
of the beating was we do not know, but it served
only to inspire new rejoicing. Even to suffer shame
for Christ was a blessing. Shame for Him was infinitely better than the honor of the world.

The more the council stamped the fire of the
gospel, the more it was fanned into new intensity—
and the more it spread. The fire could not be put
out and it would not go out by itself. It could only
grow.

5. *Seven Assistants Are Chosen (6:1-7).* As the
Jerusalem church grew larger its problems also in-

creased. The church was made up of two classes of
Jews: those who had adopted the Grecian, or Helle-
nistic, culture and those who were strict Palestinian
Jews. These were called Grecians and Hebrews. All
of them, however, were Jews—and all were now disciples of Christ. There arose suspicion and dissension
among them over the daily distribution of goods
from the common supply.

The apostles exercised wisdom in the dispute.
It was not fitting that they devote their time to this
distribution; they should better spend the time
teaching and preaching. They recommended that
the people select seven men from among themselves
who could care for the business of distribution. These
seven men must be known for their honesty, be full
of the Holy Ghost, and manifest judgment and wisdom. They were not to be merely "good fellows,"
they must be qualified to shoulder responsibility.

The seven elected to this work all have Greek
names, which strongly suggests that they were of
the Hellenist group. One, Nicholas, was even a proselyte—that is, a Gentile who had accepted the Jewish
faith. Though the word "deacon" is never used here,
it has been held from the early days of the Church
that this was the beginning of that office.

The diaconate became an important office in the
Church (1 Timothy 3:8-13), yet it is not specified
by name in the Book of Acts. Except for this fact,
which is admittedly significant, there is no reason
to believe that the appointment of the seven continued beyond the immediate local need. It was more
likely a temporary office.

The result of the increased ministry of the Word
was that many of the priests, or Sadducees, accepted

the Christian faith. Even some who had been active in the persecution were won to the faith by the persistent witness of the truth.

E. THE WITNESS AND DEATH OF STEPHEN (6:8—7:60)

Stephen, one of the seven chosen to serve tables, was an active witness of the Word. Full of faith and the Holy Ghost, he did wonders and miracles among the people. Moreover, much of Stephen's ministry centered in the synagogues frequented by the Hellenized Jews—Libertines, Cyrenians, Alexandrians, Cilicians, and Asians. These aggressive theologians disputed with Stephen but could not refute the truth of his teaching.

These Jews disputed with Stephen, but were no match for him. It is probable that in the Cilician synagogue Stephen was confronted by young Saul of Tarsus, the bright star of Judaism, fresh from the seminary of Gamaliel. But he, too, went down before Stephen.*

Unable to put Stephen down with words, the theologians then turned to brute force. They stirred up widespread hostility and had Stephen brought to trial before the Sanhedrin. There the scholars would silence Stephen. There they accused him of blasphemy against the Temple and the Law.

False witnesses quoted him as saying that Jesus of Nazareth would destroy the Temple. It is singular that this is the exact charge brought against Jesus himself by false witnesses (see Mark 14:57-59). What Jesus really said is summarized for us in John 2:19. Possibly Stephen had tried to quote Jesus

---

*A. T. Robertson, *Studies in the New Testament* (Nashville, Tennessee: Broadman Press, 1949), p. 111.

and had been misunderstood, even as Jesus himself was mis-understood.*

Stephen finally spoke in his own behalf. With face glowing like that of an angel, he preached one of the most eloquent and forceful sermons recorded in the Holy Scriptures. Stephen did not answer the accusations brought against him, nor did he try to justify his activity. Instead he gave a general survey of Hebrew history, showing how Joseph and Moses had been rejected by the ones they were born to deliver. The point was not missed by those who had so recently rejected Jesus.

Stephen also made a great point of early Jewish worship outside of Palestine. In so doing he was setting at naught the Jewish tradition that only the Temple was an appropriate place of worship. Once again his accusers did not fail to get the point. Finally, with a flaming zeal, he spoke out against the Jews with strong accusation:

Ye stiffnecked and uncircumcised in heart and ears, ye do always resist the Holy Ghost: as your fathers did, so do ye. Which of the prophets have not your fathers persecuted? and they have slain them which shewed before of the coming of the Just One; of whom ye have been now the betrayers and murderers (Acts 7:51, 52).

The Jews were so stung by these words, and the manner in which Stephen had turned history and precedence against them, that they went into a blind rage. In fury they ground their teeth at him. While the badgered Christian was surrounded by human rage and violence, God strengthened him with a vision of glory. He exclaimed on the beauty of what

*Winn, *op. cit.*, p. 57.

he saw, but the Sanhedrin, now almost berserk, stopped their ears to keep from hearing him and threw him to the ground outside the walls of the city. There they stoned him to death. The hatred of the Jews was so violent that they killed Stephen even though it was illegal for them to pass such judgment, much less carry through such an execution. In their rage the Jews lost complete control of themselves.

The spirit with which Stephen died is much like that of Christ. Still aglow with his vision, he prayed for his murderers and peacefully died. This tragic end of a dedicated, able life had one great note of eventual triumph. A young Jew from Cilicia, named Saul, was present. Eventually this young man would take up Stephen's message and carry it throughout the world.

The death of Stephen, in fact, marked a turning point in the history of the Church. Until then the faith had been confined almost entirely to Jerusalem, but Stephen's activity aroused such intense persecution that many of the disciples departed from the city. Naturally they took their faith in Christ with them. So the Church began shortly after Stephen's death to reach out beyond its cradle and begin its spread into all the world.

Witness to Judea and Samaria

Acts 8:1—12:24

A. THE DISCIPLES ARE SCATTERED (8:1-4)

Persecution both unifies and scatters the Church. It unifies in spirit and purpose; it scatters in place and grouping. For that reason even its greatest duress is often a blessing to the Church.

Thus it was with the church in Jerusalem. The effective work of the apostles and Stephen aroused the Jews to such a desperate point that they determined on the eradication of the Christian faith. This seems to have been an interim period between Roman procurators (Pilate had been recalled in disfavor to Rome) when there was no restraint of Roman law. The Jews apparently took advantage of this to take the law into their own hands. So they killed Stephen in a Jewish form of execution and launched a massive campaign of horror against all the Christians. Until now only the apostles had been arrested and imprisoned, but now every Christian was under attack.

On that very day a great storm of persecution burst upon
the Church in Jerusalem. All Church members except the
apostles were scattered over the countryside of Judaea and
Samaria. While reverent men buried Stephen and mourned
deeply over him, Saul harassed the Church bitterly. He would
go from house to house, drag out both men and women
and have them committed to prison. Those who were dispersed by his action went throughout the country, preaching
the good news of the message as they went. Philip, for instance, went down to the city of Samaria and preached Christ
to the people there. His words met with a ready and sym-
pathetic response from the large crowds who listened to him
and saw the miracles which he performed. With loud cries
evil spirits came out of those who had been possessed by
them; and many paralyzed and lame people were cured.
As a result there was great rejoicing in that city (Acts 8:1-8,
Phillips Translation).*

In the forefront of this persecution was the zealous
Pharisee from Cilicia named Saul. This Jewish fire-
brand had almost certainly confronted Stephen in
the synagogue disputes (6:9, 10); he had given his
consent (had cast his vote) for the death of Stephen
and was actually present at the execution (7:58; 8:1).

Like a wolf driven mad by the taste of blood, Saul
became a beast of prey against the Christians. He
"made havock of the church," tracking down the
men and women and casting them in prison. He
was not content to arrest those he caught in the
Temple, but invaded the homes of the Christians
and abducted those who even privately worshiped
Jesus. He became a man possessed of a lust to harass
and destroy. Many zealous Jews engaged in the persecution, but Saul outdid them all.

The persecution was so intense that all the church

---

*Op. cit.

members who escaped arrest were scattered over the countryside of Judea and Samaria. Only the apostles remained in the city. How they escaped arrest is unknown, but very likely they continued their work out of sight for the period of the persecution.

Pressure and persecution create an excellent climate for the growth of faith. The duress in Jerusalem did not stop the witness of Christ; it only scattered and increased it. The disciples who fled from the city preached the gospel everywhere they went, as even the laymen became anointed heralds of the way of Christ.

B. PHILIP'S MINISTRY IN SAMARIA (8:5-40)

1. Miracles of Philip (8:5-8). A second of the seven elected to serve tables came into prominence during the persecution. He was Philip, who went to Samaria. This was a region lying between Judea in the south and Galilee in the north. The Samaritans were a mixed people, the offspring of Jews left in Palestine during the Assyrian captivity and foreigners who migrated into the land. They were thus a race born by the admixture of Gentiles with a poor Jewish element. The higher class Jew had nothing but disdain for the Samaritans.

Though they both served Jehovah and had the same basic forms of worship, they had only hatred for each other. A common epithet among the Jews was "Thou art a Samaritan, thou hast a devil!" (John 8:48). The woman at the well reminded Jesus that "the Jews have no dealings with the Samaritans" (John 4:9).

Jesus made a great point of accepting the Samaritans and resisting the prejudice against them. He made a Samaritan the good neighbor, as compared with a Jewish Levite and priest, in the Parable of the Good Samaritan (Luke 10:33). It is recorded that out of ten only one, a Samaritan, returned to thank Jesus when they were healed of leprosy (Luke 17:15, 16). He freely violated Jewish custom by passing through Samaria on His journeys (Luke 9:52).

The most important contact Jesus had with the Samaritans was when He passed through their land early in His ministry (John 4:3-43). During the two days He stayed in the province and preached to them, many Samaritans believed and accepted Him as the Messiah (John 4:29, 39, 41, 42). The results amounted to a revival among the despised people.

Good seed had been sown in Samaria, and Philip went to reap the harvest. This was a break with the harshly-etched racial pattern of the Jews. Because he had a burden for souls on his heart, Philip refused to be hindered by unreasoning prejudices. His ministry was highly effective, his words were convincing, and the miracles he performed affirmed the gospel of Christ. A great revival resulted, so much that the whole city was made aware of the spreading faith of Christ. As always, the gospel was accompanied by joy in the hearts of those who received it.

2. *Simon the Sorcerer (8:9-25).* Not all of those in Samaria, however, were happy about the revival. One such person was a man called Simon, a skilled magician who had convinced the Samaritans that he possessed divine power. The things he pretended to do paled in comparison with the true deeds of power Philip did in the name of Jesus. Simon saw his hold on the people slipping. More than that, he

became confused himself. Convinced that the works of Philip were real, since he could not duplicate them with his trickery, he followed Philip and watched him closely. He even came to have a kind of faith—probably no more than mental assent to the gospel—and was baptized. With all this he still could not do the things Philip did.

Somehow word reached the apostles—who had stayed in Jerusalem despite the persecution—about the revival in Samaria. They sent Peter and John to assist Philip in his work. The two apostles joined in heartily and prayed that the Samaritan converts might also receive the Holy Ghost. Through their prayers and the laying on of their hands, the believers received the deeper experience just as the 120 had received it on the Day of Pentecost.

In this instance there is a clear and distinct separation between the work of salvation by faith and the baptism of the Holy Ghost. The Samaritans received the word of God, believed, were baptized, and then received the Holy Ghost. This is the procedure to this day. First the believer receives salvation; then, and only then, is he eligible to receive the Holy Ghost. The pattern was consistent throughout the Book of Acts.

While the phenomenon of speaking in tongues mentioned in 2:4, 10:46 and 19:6 is not mentioned here, it is strongly implied. Something happened that Simon could observe when the believers received the Holy Ghost: "Simon saw that through laying on of the apostles' hands the Holy Ghost was given" (8:18). Consistency with every other instance of Holy Ghost outpouring would mean that this conspicuous manifestation was speaking with tongues.

Still confused and frustrated by all he saw, Simon tried to buy the power of the Holy Ghost. Peter set the sorcerer straight in no uncertain terms:

Thy money perish with thee, because thou hast thought that the gift of God may be purchased with money. Thou hast neither part nor lot in this matter: for thy heart is not right in the sight of God (Acts 8:20, 21).

Peter strongly hinted that the magician's iniquity came close to being a sin against the Holy Ghost (8:22, 23), for which there is no forgiveness (Mark 3:28, 29). Simon's perverted nature and devilish ambition had brought him not to the gate of eternal life but near the pit of damnation. So it is with all who trifle with holy things or mix the holy with the profane. Divine power cannot be controlled or manipulated by the vagaries of human desire.

3. *The Ethiopian Eunuch (8:26-40).* Led by the angel of the Lord, Philip went southward along the desert road between Jerusalem and Gaza. There he encountered an Ethiopian who had been in Jerusalem for worship. He was evidently a proselyte to the Jewish faith. Ethiopia was an ancient kingdom on the edge of the Nubian Desert. The people were dark-skinned, distinctly Negroid in their features and characteristics. Yet the faith of Israel had been known in the land since the days of Solomon.

Philip joined the Ethiopian treasurer, a eunuch, in his chariot, which was probably a covered carriage for court travel, not an open war chariot. As the two men rode along Philip observed that the Ethiopian was reading Isaiah 53 (though the Bible was not then divided into chapters). Isaiah 53 is a direct prophecy of Jesus, so Philip used this as his opening to preach Christ to the eunuch.

The Ethiopian was ready for the gospel. Just as the Holy Spirit led Philip to the chariot, the Spirit had also prepared the heart of the eunuch. While the evangelist spoke, the eager seeker believed unto salvation and desired baptism. Providentially they came to a pool of water—probably an oasis—near the road they traveled. Here we see how the Early Church baptized its converts. They both went into the pool, and Philip committed the new convert to the water in baptism.

Both men were overcome with joy. The Ethiopian went on his way rejoicing, and Philip, caught away by the Spirit, went into Azotus. This was the ancient Philistine city of Ashdod, near the Mediterannean coast. There Philip preached the gospel from village to village as he made his way north to Caesarea. He apparently settled in Caesarea, for we hear of him in that coastal city many years later (21:8).

As for the Ethiopian, there is a tradition that he returned to his country and evangelized his people. Modern Ethiopia to this day calls itself the oldest Christian kingdom of the African continent.

C. THE EMERGENCE OF SAUL OF TARSUS (9:1-31)

1. Saul's Hatred of the Christians (9:1, 2). Saul was a young theologian from Tarsus, a Roman city in the province of Cilicia, in Asia Minor. Saul had come to Jerusalem to study in the school of Gamaliel. The young man had the stamp of greatness upon him. As a citizen of Tarsus and the son of a free man, Saul enjoyed Roman citizenship with all its advantages (22:26-38). He was thoroughly Hellenized, learned in the Greek arts and sciences. But, above all, he was ardently Jewish in his religion. A dedicated Pharisee, he was a scholar of the Law of Moses and a zealot for its enforcement.

Saul, however, became a beast of prey, a wolf with the taste of blood in his mouth. He very likely engaged in the disputes with Stephen and thereupon became incensed against the Christian faith. He came to regard the disciples' message as the rankest heresy and devoted his vast energy and genius to stamping it out. It appears that his paramount grievance against the Christians was the manner in which the One they worshiped had died. Jesus of Nazareth had died on a cross, and the Jewish Law stated that "cursed is every one that hangeth on a tree" (Galatians 3:13; Deuteronomy 21:23). Not only had Jesus died on a tree, but on a despised Roman tree at that. It was clear to Saul that Jesus had died with the curse of God upon Him. How then did these blasphemers dare to call Him the Son of God?

Saul came to have a fierce hatred for those who worshiped Jesus. He put many into prison, invading the privacy of Christian homes and showing no mercy even to the women (8:3). He "persecuted this way unto the death, binding and delivering into prisons both men and women" (22:4). The manner in which Saul persecuted the Church is mentioned at least nine times in the Scriptures—seven by Paul (as he was later called) himself.

He "made havock of the church" (8:3).

He breathed out "threatenings and slaughter" (9:1).

He "persecuted this way unto the death" (22:4).

He "beyond measure . . . persecuted the church of God, and wasted it" (Galatians 1:13).

He called himself "a blasphemer, and a persecutor" (1 Timothy 1:13).

Probably the most comprehensive summary of Saul's savagery against the Church is found in his own speech to King Agrippa: "I verily thought with myself, that I ought to do many things contrary to the name of Jesus of Nazareth. Which thing I also did in Jerusalem: and many of the saints did *I shut up in prison,* having received authority from the chief priests; and when they were *put to death,* I gave my voice against them. And I *punished them oft* in every synagogue, and *compelled them to blaspheme;* and being exceedly mad against them, I persecuted them even unto strange cities" (Acts 26:9-11).

How he caused the Christians to blaspheme is not stated. Very likely he forced them to renounce Christ on pain of death. Many died rather than deny Christ, but some probably failed God under the terrifying menace of Saul. The fact that he "gave his voice" against the Christians means that he voted against them. This implies that he was a member of the Sanhedrin and had a vote in such matters.

Saul had become abductor, prosecutor, judge, and executioner of the followers of Christ. It is hard for us today to imagine such a cruel obsession in anyone. But when a person of culture and cultivation, of refinement and breeding, a person of religious conviction becomes possessed of a fury and a wrath, the situation is ripe for destruction and carnage.

Determined upon destroying the Christian faith,

Saul first imprisoned all he could of that faith in
Jerusalem. (At this time the apostles were in the
city, but they escaped detection.) When he had suf-
ficiently achieved his purpose, the arrogant young
Jew pressed his cause into other cities.

His ready admittance to the high priest and his
success in securing warrants for the arrest of the
Christians indicate that Saul was a person of considerable importance and rank among the priests
and elders. The leaders of Israel were no doubt happy to see someone of such zeal and ability ready
to pursue such a cause for them.

2. *The Conversion of Saul (9:3-19)*. With his letters from the high priest Saul set out for Damascus.
This Syrian city had a large colony of Jews, among
whom were many who had accepted Christ. The
brilliant but angry young man had a lust for their
blood and pressed his journey forward with eagerness. The distance between Jerusalem and Damascus
was about 160 miles, about a six-day journey.

On the last day of the journey, when only a long
stretch of desert separated Saul from his prey, a wonderful thing happened. He was overcome by a daz-
zling light that shone from heaven. The Chief Shepherd of the little flock struck the mad wolf to the
ground. While he lay trembling in the sand, the
Shepherd pulled out the wolf's fangs and turned
him into the meekest lamb of the fold.

When Jesus spoke to Saul He made it clear that
it was He whom Saul had persecuted. That Saul was
already suffering in his conscience because of his
cruel deeds is intimated by the statement: "It is hard
for thee to kick against the pricks." The force that
struck Saul down was so great that his companions

fell also (20:14). These men were able to hear the sound of Saul and Jesus as they spoke (9:7), but they did not understand the meaning (22:9).

While Saul lay on the ground he was changed. There he saw that the curse Jesus bore on the cross belonged not to Jesus, but to him and all mankind (Galatians 3:13). He saw the magnitude of his sin, and that his sin was more than equaled by the magnitude of God's love. Saul not only accepted the fact that Jesus had died on a cross, but while he lay on the ground he died on his cross with Jesus.

I am crucified with Christ: nevertheless I live; yet not I, but Christ liveth in me: and the life which I now live in the flesh I live by the faith of the Son of God, who loved me, and gave himself for me (Galatians 2:20).

Saul was led blind into the city he had intended to enter as a persecutor and inquisitor. In his feeble state he fasted and prayed for three days. But God was already working in his behalf. Ananias, leader of the Damascus church, was directed in a vision to go to Saul. The transformation of Saul was completed when Ananias received him into the Christian fellowship. Saul received the Holy Ghost, was healed of his blindness, and was baptized.

The course God had ordained for Saul was revealed to Ananias during the period of Saul's blindness: "He is a chosen vessel unto me, to bear my name before the Gentiles, and kings, and the children of Israel." Later, the Lord said, "I will shew him [Saul] how great things he must suffer for my name's sake."

Hereafter the life of Saul would be bound up with the Name he had so ardently hated. He would love, suffer, and even die for that Name. No greater miracle has ever been wrought.

3. Saul Begins to Preach (9:20-31). The energies of Saul were immediately turned to the cause of Christ. He began to preach in the synagogues of Damascus that Jesus was the Son of God. The Jews were amazed at Saul's change of purpose and direction. To them he seemed a traitor, for he now espoused the cause he had so recently tried to stamp out. He now had fellowship with those he had come to arrest. He had volunteered for this hateful task, but now he would not fulfill it.

The Jews, who could not refute his words, resorted to attempts to kill him. The Damascus disciples, whose lives he so recently would have taken, now helped him save his own.

By following only the Book of Acts our picture of this period is incomplete. Galatians 1:16-27 and 2 Corinthians 11:32, 33 must be reconciled with the narrative in Acts. But that is not easy, for the references are not detailed. A possible reconstruction of the period is as follows:

1. Saul preaches in Damascus (9:20, 21)
2. He goes into Arabia (Galatians 1:17)
3. He returns to Damascus (9:23-25; Galatians 1:17; 2 Corinthians 11:32, 33)
4. After three years in Damascus, he then goes to Jerusalem (9:26-29)

When Saul went to Jerusalem, the disciples were still afraid of him. The persecution fomented by him was a fresh and painful memory to them. Barnabas however, was willing to take a chance with him. This son of consolation accepted Paul and took him to the apostles. From Galatians 1:18, 19 we know that he saw only Peter and James, the brother of Jesus. He stayed with the disciples for fifteen days and worked among them. Then he went into Caesarea, whence he sailed for Tarsus in Cilicia. That was home. There Saul would remain several years before we hear of him again.

D. FURTHER MINISTRY OF PETER
   (9:32—11:18)

1. *Healing of Aeneas and Dorcas (9:32-43)*. The scene shifts once again to Peter. The apostle went out from Jerusalem to preach among the bands of disciples springing up throughout Judea. In Lydda Aeneas, who had been afflicted for eight years, was healed instantly.

Then Peter was called to Joppa on the seacoast, where Dorcas, a woman of great charity, had died and was laid out for burial. The affection the bereaved friends had for Dorcas was very touching as they showed Peter proofs of her good deeds. Peter sent everyone from the room, and in faith and undisturbed concentration he prayed. Dorcas was raised from the dead, the first to be so raised by an apostle.

Peter stayed in Joppa for many days as a guest in the home of a tanner named Simon. While there God led Peter into another sphere of the Christian witness.

2. *Cornelius Becomes a Christian (10:1-48)*. This section of Acts is of great importance to the Christian faith. It marks the departure of the apostles from their strictly Jewish ministry. Until this time they

had conceived of their task as being primarily to the "house of Israel." Jesus had told them, however, that they were to bear witness beyond the Jewish nation (1:8). This was a serious departure from all previous concepts, so it could have begun only by direct leading of the Spirit.

This direction of the Spirit came appropriately to Simon Peter; it was ordained that he should introduce the Christian faith to the Gentiles just as he had introduced it to the Jews at Pentecost. In Caesarea, a seaport named for the Roman Caesar and occupied by a Roman garrison, there was a God-fearing man from Italy named Cornelius. Though this man was a commander of the Roman army (a centurion was an officer with a hundred men under his command), he was a devout, prayerful, and charitable man. He worshiped the true God of the Jews, not the heathen gods of Rome. He faithfully observed the Jewish hours of prayer (10:3, 30), yet he clearly was not a Jewish proselyte. Cornelius was of such spiritual mien that God sent an angel who called his name and spoke directly to him.

"Cornelius . . . thy prayers and thine alms are come up for a memorial before God." The centurion was directed to send for Simon Peter, who was still abiding in Joppa with Simon the tanner. God had prepared Peter for the occasion by giving him a vision of God's acceptance of the Gentile people (10:9-16). In his divine way God prepared one to receive the message and another to give it.

At first Peter did not understand the dream of unclean beasts made clean by the Lord. When the messengers of Cornelius spoke to him, he then understood that the beasts represented the Gentiles.

They were to hear the gospel also.

Peter went to Cornelius, though it was against Jewish custom to do so (10:28), and accepted the Gentile into the Christian faith. It is strongly suggested that Cornelius and his house were already aware of the Christian gospel (verse 37), but their knowledge was incomplete. Peter's message was a confirmation as well as a revelation to their hearts. What the Gentiles had heard about Christ the apostles could affirm because they had been "eye witnesses." Peter's sermon confirmed the Gentiles' exercise of faith so that the full work of Christ was done in their hearts.

The message of Peter was interrupted by the outpouring of the Holy Ghost (10:44). The Gentiles also spoke in tongues when they received the Holy Ghost. The Jews had received the experience (2:4); the Samaritans had received it (8:15-17); and now the Gentiles received it (10:44-46). The promise was indeed "unto you, and to your children, and to all that are afar off, even as many as the Lord our God shall call" (2:39).

3. *Peter Defends His Ministry to the Gentiles (11:1-18).* News of Peter's ministry to Cornelius received a mixed reaction in Jerusalem. The Christians rejoiced to hear of further spread of the gospel, but they were also disquieted by the fact that it was to Gentiles. Gentiles could become Jews by submitting themselves to the rite of circumcision—these were called proselytes—but Cornelius had not done this. *His faith in the Jewish God was without his conformity to the Jewish rituals.* He was an out-and-out Gentile. And Peter had dared to enter his house

and eat with him. So when Peter came again to
Jerusalem he was challenged by the Jewish Christians for his action.

The particular point would later become a great
issue in the Church and would be interpreted by
an appropriate council (15:1, 5-11, 24-31). At the
time of Peter's report, however, there was no thought
except that Gentiles were not eligible for the gospel.
Peter defended his action by relating all the details
to the brethren. He used three points to justify his
going to Cornelius and to prove that God's grace
had been extended to Gentile as well as Jew. He
told how God had given him the vision illustrating
the Gentiles' right to hear the Word, how this was
confirmed by an angel's appearance to Cornelius,
and how the Holy Ghost had come upon the Gentiles.

Peter's three points of confirmation could not be
denied or ignored. God Himself had prepared the
way for Gentiles to enter the fold; Peter had only
opened the door at His bidding.

Upon hearing these things, there was nothing the
apostles and brethren could say. They could not
withstand God any more than Peter had done (11:17).
They could only praise God that the Gentiles were
also granted repentance unto life.

E. THE CHURCH IN ANTIOCH (11:19-26)

One of the blessings of the persecution following
Stephen's death was the dispersion of the Christians
to distant cities. As we have already seen, some went
to Damascus. Others went to such places as the coast
of Phoenicia and the island of Cyprus. Some went

to Antioch, the capital of Syria. This was an important city, the third largest in the Roman Empire, surpassed only by Rome and Alexandria.

Antioch was to play a great role in the affairs of the church. It was there that the gospel was deliberately preached to the Gentiles. What Peter had done to the household of Cornelius on a special occasion, and at the invitation of Cornelius, disciples from Cyprus and Cyrene began to do in Antioch regularly and of their own initiative: They preached the gospel to Gentiles.

This was a new thing. Frequently Gentiles who sought admission to the Jewish faith were admitted by the Jews. But it was not a common thing. Here, however, the Church actually went out and sought the Gentiles.

Antioch, with the Mediterranean Sea only fifteen miles to the west and the Seleucid (Greek) Empire to the north, naturally had a large Greek population. So while the Palestinian Christians preached to their fellow Jews, the Cypriot and Cyrenian Christians preached to the Greeks. They methodically and purposefully sought to convert the Greeks to Christ. This was a noble and decisive venture. The Church would never be the same again.

Two things happened that affected the Christian faith permanently and kept it from becoming a mere sect of the Jews. First, the center of operations gradually shifted from Jerusalem to Antioch. For any city outside of Palestine even to share the spotlight with Jerusalem was a new thing. Jerusalem had from time immemorial been like a mother to all Jews everywhere. It would remain important to the Church as a home base, but never again would it

be the unrivaled center of Christian operation as
it had been of Jewish operation.

Second, the Church would never again be an ex-
clusively Jewish movement. Hereafter, its message
would be directed also to the Gentiles. Considerable
opposition to this would remain, but the motion
was started, and its movement would never be halted.
Instead, it would increase until Jew and Gentile
would be equal. In time to come the Gentiles would
become predominant, and Christianity would flow
its separate way from Judaism. Though this would
one day be the general course of the Church, the
direction was set in Antioch. This was the beginning
of the trickle.

Upon hearing of the revival in Antioch, the church
in Jerusalem sent Barnabas to direct and supervise
it. Barnabas by this time had gained considerable
stature in the church. It is possible that he was sent
to Antioch because he was a Cypriot and those who
were preaching to the Greeks were his countrymen.

What Barnabas saw in Antioch impressed him
as being the God-directed course. He joined in the
revival with heart and might. He went to Tarsus
and sought the young Saul to come to Antioch to
help him. It was time now for Saul to begin his massive labors, and who more than gentle Barnabas—
good, and full of the Holy Ghost—could lead the
young man forth and initiate him into the labor
of the Lord. This was the beginning of a fruitful
association, for these two men would labor together
as witnesses of Christ "into all the world."

Antioch was a turning point for the Church in
still another way: It was there that the disciples were
first called Christians (11:26). Until then the follow-

ers of Christ were called "disciples," which meant "pupils" or "learners." The faith of Christ was simply called "The Way." Very likely the term *Christian* was first coined in derision or mockery, for such names are usually begun in this fashion.

The word Christian occurs only three times in the New Testament (Acts 11:26; 26:28; and 1 Peter 4:16). The first passage, Acts 11:26, gives the origin of the term, "The disciples were called Christians first in Antioch." . . . A Christian is thus simply an adherent of Christ. The name belongs, as Ramsay says, to the popular slang, as indeed sect and party names generally do. It is only after a considerable interval, and very often under protest, that such names are accepted as self-designations.

The name, then, did not originate with the Christians themselves. Nor would the Jews have applied it to the followers of Jesus, whose claim to be the Christ they opposed so passionately. They spoke of the Christians as "the sect of the Nazarenes" (Acts 24:5); perhaps also as "Galileans," a term which the emperior Julian attempted later vainly to revive. The word must have been coined by the heathen population of Antioch, as the church emerged from the synagogue, and a Christianity predominantly gentile took its place among the religions of the world.[*]

F. SUFFERINGS OF THE JERUSALEM CHURCH (11:27—12:24)

1. Relief Sent From Antioch (11:27-30). A great fellowship existed between the churches in Jerusalem and Antioch. Prophets went from the older church in Judea to the younger in Syria and helped to establish and strengthen the new Antiochian Christians. It developed in another way, however, that Antioch

---

[*]John Dickie, "Christian," *International Standard Bible Encyclopedia* (James Orr, ed., Grand Rapids, Michigan: William B. Eerdmans Publishing Company), I, p. 621.

was able to assist Jerusalem. Agabus, one of the men from Jerusalem, in an utterance of prophecy, revealed that a great famine was imminent. This soon came to pass.

The famine seems to have been extremely severe in Judea. The suffering there was sufficient to arouse the sympathy of the church in Antioch. In a beautiful example of Christian charity, the church sent Barnabas and Saul with assistance to their Judean brethren.

This famine is also mentioned by Josephus *(Antiquities* xx.2.5.) as being so severe it caused the death of many inhabitants of Judea. It appears that the period of dearth lasted three or four years.

2. Martyrdom of James (12:1, 2). Somewhere about the time Barnabas and Saul took the relief from Antioch to Judea (11:30) a new wave of persecution swept Jerusalem. Herod the king put forth violent hands against the leaders of the Church. He beheaded James the apostle.

This was Herod Agrippa, son of Aristobulus and grandson of Herod the Great. By his deeds it can be seen that much of the evil Herodian strain was still in him. For a brief period Palestine did not have the presence of Roman Law and was left in the hands of its own rulers as it had been at the death of Stephen. Herod ruled in the name of Rome as king over all Palestine.

There was no portion of time for thirty years before, or ever afterward, in which there was a king at Jerusalem, a person exercising that authority in Judea, or to whom that title could be applied, except the last three years of Herod's life, within which period the transaction here recorded took place.*

James was the first of the Twelve to be martyred—the only one whose death is recorded in the Scriptures, though tradition relates that all save John were martyred. This James was the brother of John, of whom we read much in the Gospels.

The James of whom we hear much in the following portions of Acts was the brother of the Lord (Galatians 1:19), frequently spoken of as James the Less.

3. Peter Imprisoned and Delivered (12:3-19). The beheading of James pleased the Jews. When Herod Agrippa saw this, he decided on a further gesture of oppression. Peter was to be the next victim. The obvious intention was to make a public spectacle of Peter's execution.

It was the Passover season (called Easter here) however, so the execution was delayed until the seven days of unleavened bread were over. Peter was put in prison, guarded by four groups of four soldiers. These sixteen guards divided the night into four watches so that four were on duty at all times. This security would surely make escape impossible. But Herod Agrippa did not take the power of God into consideration. God easily makes mockery of man's best efforts.

During the days of Peter's imprisonment the church did not cease to pray for him (12:5), but

*Horatio B. Hackett, *A Commentary on the Acts of the Apostles,* Vol. IV of *An American Commentary on the New Testament* (Alvah Hovey, ed., Philadelphia: The American Baptist Publication Society, 1882), p. 143.

God waited until the night before Peter's public
execution to intervene. One more night and then
the bloodthirsty spectators would be gratified. Peter
would be killed and Herod would be even more
popular with the religious leaders. But Herod was
nearer his death than Peter was to his.

The angel of God delivered Peter from the prison
by performing a remarkable series of miracles. The
guards were put into a deep sleep or otherwise in-
capacitated. The prison doors were opened. The
city gates opened of their own accord. The whole
deliverance was so incredible that even Peter had
to collect his wits before he fully realized what had
happened (vv. 9, 11, 12). When he reached John
Mark's house where the Christians were praying,
they could not readily believe their eyes. It was a
thing too good to be true.

Peter reported to James and the brethren, and
then "departed and went into another place." This
probably means that he left Jerusalem for a time,
knowing what a stir would be created when his escape
was discovered.

4. The Death of Herod (12:20-23). Herod Agrippa
went from Jerusalem to Caesarea to preside over
a series of public functions in honor of Claudius,
the Roman Caesar. The cities of Tyre and Sidon,
which were in dispute with Herod concerning trade
agreements, sent a delegation to Caesarea to nego-
tiate with him. Tyre and Sidon were Phoenician
coastal cities, depending on their far-ranging ships
for trade and commerce. They traded their merchan-
dise for grain from Palestine's inland fields. To pre-
serve the economic stability of their cities, which

the displeasure of Herod threatened to upset, the delegation arranged a meeting with the king.

Herod met the Phoenicians in his resplendent royal robes and during the negotiations made a public speech. It appears that an agreement was reached and that Herod's speech concerned the restored peace between the two lands. The king's eloquence so stirred the people that they acclaimed his voice to be the voice of a god. The significance of this was that the people, who were mostly heathen, hailed Herod as a god rather than a man.

When the impious king accepted the acclaim instead of turning it to the glory of God, the angel of the Lord smote the proud, cruel man with a foul disease. According to Josephus he lingered in horrible agony for five days before dying.

5. *Transition to Antioch (12:24, 25)*. The death of Herod introduced a new period of peace and growth to the Church. About this time Barnabas and Saul returned to Antioch, bringing John Mark with them. Hereafter, Antioch, not Jerusalem, would provide the main thrust of the gospel into other parts of the world.

The witnesses had gone out from Jerusalem into Judea and Samaria and beyond. Jew, Samaritan, Ethiopian, Roman, and Greek had received the witness. Now the door of the world was open and it was time for the gospel to go from Antioch to the uttermost part of the earth.

Witness to the World

Acts 13:1—21:17

A. PAUL'S FIRST MISSIONARY JOURNEY (13:1—14:28)

1. Barnabas and Saul Are Sent Forth (13:1-5). Antioch became the mother church of Gentile Christianity. The broad geographic base of its congregation fitted it for this ministry. Barnabas, the senior minister, was from Cyprus; Simeon was probably from Africa; Lucius was from Cyrene; Manaen had been educated with Herod the tetrarch; Saul, the youngest leader, was from Cilicia. These men were acquainted with a Gentile society. Fittingly, it was they who were led of the Holy Ghost to launch the first extensive missionary endeavor. Barnabas and Saul were sent forth by their brethren to evangelize distant parts of the world.

It is unlikely that those who laid hands on Barnabas and Saul knew where the Spirit would lead them. It was enough that the Holy Ghost had said, "Separate ME Barnabas and Saul for the work *whereunto I have* called them." This was one of the most important calls which has ever come to the Church. It was the beginning of a new outreach. Human planning did not initiate the new step, but it was part of a divine plan.

Barnabas and Saul went to Seleucia, a seaport near Antioch, whence they sailed a hundred miles west to the island of Cyprus. The two companions took John Mark along with them. Exactly what this young man's duties were is not stated, but it is likely that he assisted in the evangelistic endeavors, though not in any prominent manner. Some think that he merely cared for the incidental needs of Barnabas and Saul.

2. Opposition on Cyprus (13:6-13). The missionary party crossed the island of Cyprus, from Salamis on the eastern shore to Paphos on the western, a distance of about a hundred miles. In Paphos the Roman deputy of the country, Sergius Paulus, showed a genuine interest in Christianity. But a Jewish sorcerer, Elymas, who was attached to the deputy as a religious advisor, wielded considerable influence over him. Foreseeing a loss of his personal influence and advantages if the governor accepted the Christian faith, this evil magician actively withstood the gospel and undertook to persuade Sergius Paulus against it.

This was a pattern of things to come. When Gentiles were inclined toward the faith of Christ, the Jews, whose spiritual heritage should have made them the foremost advocates of the Messianic message, both resisted and hindered the Word of God.

The result of Elymas' interference was quick and startling.

Saul became inflamed in spirit toward the sorcerer's obstructive efforts. Under the anointing of the Holy Spirit, the apostle fixed his piercing eyes upon

Elymas and assailed him as the "child of the devil."
Then this practitioner of the black arts was struck
blind so that the blackness of his eyes could match
the blackness of his soul.

It is here that the change of name from Saul to
Paul was first noted (v. 9). The change was simply
one of form and has no actual spiritual significance.
Paul is the Greek form of the Hebrew Saul. Among
the Jews in Palestine the Hebrew Saul was used,
but as soon as Paul went out from Palestine, the
Greek form was adopted.

Another point of interest is seen in this section.
At the outset of their partnership, Barnabas was
mentioned first, then Paul. Almost immediately,
however, the leadership of Paul became apparent.
Perhaps the difference in the two men's dispositions
was best dramatized in their reaction to the case of
Elymas. Barnabas was doubtlessly equally concerned,
but Paul did something about it. He had to. He was
a man of bold, decisive action. Hereafter the partnership would be referred to as Paul and Barnabas.

So they were "Paul and his company" when they
departed from Cyprus to Perga, a city of Pamphilia
on the coast of Asia Minor.

John Mark left the missionaries in Pamphylia and
returned to his home in Jerusalem. We do not know
why he deserted the group, but we know that it
greatly agitated Paul, for the apostle would remem-
ber it with displeasure in time to come (15:38). It
is commonly thought that Mark became frightened
when he saw what hardships and opposition the
Christian band must face. He was a young man, and
others have suggested that he simply became home-
sick for his mother. Still others feel that he, being

the nephew of Barnabas, observed and resented the transition of leadership from Barnabas to Paul.

3. In Antioch of Pisidia (13:14-43). Paul and Barnabas did not stay in Perga long enough to preach there. Instead, they pressed across the high Taurus Mountains to Antioch in Pisidia. Antioch, which is not to be confused with the Syrian Antioch, was situated in the high plateau region of Pisidia. As a Roman colony, it had many foreigners as well as its own natives, including a Jewish community. Because of the Dispersion, Jews were in most parts of the world, and wherever they had sufficient numbers, they established their synagogues. Paul always used this situation to the advantage of the gospel. When he went to a city he went first to the synagogue and preached. As a recognized Jewish rabbi he had a right to speak and be heard. Furthermore, the congregations were usually glad to receive a visiting rabbi. There Paul was able to preach to the people that the Christ of God had come, Jesus of Nazareth.

So it was in Antioch of Pisidia. The rulers of the synagogue invited the visitors to speak a word of exhortation. Paul preached. The statement that he beckoned with his hand suggests that he spoke with emphasis and gestures to drive home his points. He addressed himself to both the Jews, "men of Israel," and Gentiles, "ye that fear God." These Gentiles, who sat in a separate part of the synagogue, were the ripe field of evangelism.

Paul preached a great sermon tracing the life of Christ as the seed of David. This Jesus, whom the authorities at Jerusalem rejected, was the Son of God. The people were so affected by the sermon that

they followed after the apostles to hear more from
them and urged Paul to speak again the next Sab-
bath (13:42, 43). Some of the people seem to have
been converted, for they were encouraged to "continue in the grace of God."

4. Paul Turns to the Gentiles (13:44-52). Paul's
first sermon so stirred the people that almost the
entire city gathered to hear him the following Sab-
bath. With such city-wide interest it is likely that
both Paul and Barnabas were busy preaching.

The pattern of Jewish opposition continued. Jeal-
ous of the popularity of the Apostles, the Jews, under
the goading of their rabbis, became hostile.

Nothing is specifically stated here about the rabbis, but
they were beyond doubt the instigators of, and the ring-
leaders in, the opposition as in Thessalonica (17:5).[*]

The tension became more and more pronounced
until at last it reached the breaking point. But the
breaking point was also a turning point. If the Jews
would not receive the gospel, Paul and Barnabas
would leave the synagogue.

And Paul and Barnabas spake out boldly, and said, It
was necessary that the word of God should first be spoken
to you. Seeing ye thrust it from you, and judge yourselves
unworthy of eternal life, lo, we turn to the Gentiles. For
so hath the Lord commanded us, saying, I have set thee for
a light of the Gentiles, That thou shouldest be for salvation
unto the uttermost part of the earth (Acts 13:46, 47, *American
Standard Version*).

The Jews had proved themselves unworthy of sal-

---

[*]A. T. Robertson, *Word Pictures in the New Testament*, Vol. III:
The Acts of the Apostles (New York: Harper & Brothers, 1930), p. 197.

vation. Though the apostles had preached first to
the Jews, they had spurned their opportunity. Finally
Paul and Barnabas shook the dust from their feet
as a gesture of contempt against the persecution they
received. In Matthew 10:14 the Lord had commanded such action as a judgment against those who as-
saulted the gospel (Matthew 10:14).

Henceforth, in Antioch they would preach to the
Gentiles. In other places Paul would go to the Jews,
where they would receive him, but not here. The
result was a great spreading of the gospel among
the Gentiles and persecution from the Jews.

Opposition, however, did not discourage the new
Gentile Christians in Antioch. Their faith was like
a nail—the harder the Jews hit it the more firmly
they drove it in. The Gentiles were "glad, and glorified the word of the Lord." Furthermore, "the word
of the Lord was published throughout all the region"
and "the disciples were filled with joy and with the
Holy Ghost" (13:48, 52).

5. *Farther Into Galatia (14:1-18).* In Iconium, a
city sixty miles southeast of Antioch of Pisidia, Paul
and Barnabas also preached in the synagogue of the
Jews. The results were much as they had been in
Antioch: When many Jews and Gentiles believed,
the unbelieving Jews began to stir up trouble. Soon
the whole city of Iconium was in division over the
matter. The city finally reached a point of riot, and
the rabbis led a mob against the apostles to humiliate
them and to stone them.

Prudently, Paul and Barnabas fled to Lystra and
Derbe, adjoining cities in the province of Lycaonia,
twenty miles southeast of Iconium. And there "they

preached the gospel" (v. 7).

In Lystra we have the first record of a healing in Paul's ministry. A lame man was healed and a strange response resulted: When the lame man leaped up and the people of Lystra saw the miracle, their pagan minds came to a natural conclusion: Paul and Barnabas were gods!

The superstitious people mistook Barnabas for Jupiter, and Paul for Mercurius (Mercury). In ancient mythology Jupiter was chief of the gods, aloof and majestic; Mercury was the god of eloquence and speed. Thus Barnabas, older and possibly more commanding in appearance, was hailed as Jupiter, while Paul, eloquent and younger, was called Mercury.

Observing this development, the pagan priest thought it best not to dispute it but to capitalize on it. Only when the priest led a joyful procession of worshipers and sacrificial oxen toward them were the apostles able to comprehend what was going on. Evidently they did not understand the Lycaonian language. Finally comprehending, the apostles ran among the people and put a halt to the proceedings.

6. *Paul Is Stoned (14:19, 20).* The Jewish leaders hounded Paul and Barnabas all the way across the vast province of Galatia. Especially angry with Paul, they came from Pisidian Antioch and Iconium to stir up new trouble for the apostles. This time he did not escape. The angry mob stoned Paul and dragged his battered body to the outskirts of Lystra. Barnabas likely escaped because he was now less conspicuous and less offensive to the Jews than Paul. But the converts to the faith stood round about the body of Paul. Some have suggested that they stood

grieving; others that they gathered to bury him. It is much more in keeping with the mood of the account and the Christian spirit that they were praying for his recovery.

And Paul did recover. He arose and went back into Lystra. Because Lystra was the home of the devout family of Timothy, a young man who was to become Paul's companion, it is likely that Paul dwelt there during his recovery.

7. *Revisitation and Homegoing (14:21-28).* Derbe was the end of the route for the missionaries. They retraced their steps from there, visiting again the disciples in Lystra, Iconium, and Antioch. They established the churches in the rugged heartland of Galatia, ordaining elders in every city.

Then Paul and Barnabas returned to Antioch in Syria.

B. THE COUNCIL IN JERUSALEM (15:1-35)

Chapter 15 is one of the most important chapters of the Book of Acts. It tells how the Church came to the brink of schism, and how the orderly, spiritual process of counsel preserved it from disaster.

The trouble began when old-line Jews from Judea, who were now Christians, made a great issue over circumcision. They insisted that even the Gentiles who were converted to Christ must come by way of Judaism. This meant in particular that they must be circumcised. The more liberal Jews from Antioch held opposite views. They felt that Gentiles could come directly to Christ and that the rite of circumcision was now of little significance. The experiences of Paul and Barnabas had demonstrated this to be

true, so the Antiochians sent the two apostles to
Jerusalem to confer with the Twelve and the elders.
The issue was of such magnitude and significance
that additional delegates also went from Antioch.
According to Galatians 2:1-10, Titus was one of those.
Titus was a Greek, and uncircumcised, so he may
well have been sent as an exhibit of God's free grace
to the Gentiles.

Paul and Barnabas privately related to the apostles
and elders what God had done in the Gentile lands.
Then a group of ex-Pharisees rose up to demand that
all Gentiles be circumcised before being accepted
into the fellowship of the Church. This threw the
matter into full-scale public meetings.

> These ex-Pharisees were the same whom Paul, in the
> heat of controversy, more severely calls "false brethren
> insidiously or stealthily foisted in," who intruded them-
> selves into the Christian brotherhood as spies and enemies
> of Christian liberty. He clearly distinguishes them not
> only from the apostles, but also from the great majority
> of the brethren in Judea who sincerely rejoiced in his
> conversion and glorified God for it. They were a small,
> but very active and zealous minority, and full of intrigue.
> They compassed sea and land to make one proselyte.
> They were baptized with water, but not with the Holy
> Spirit. They were Christians in name, but narrow-minded
> and narrow-hearted Jews in fact. They were scrupulous,
> pedantic, slavish formalists, ritualists, and traditionalists
> of the malignant type. Circumcision of the flesh was to
> them of more importance than circumcision of the heart,
> or at all events an indispensable condition of salvation.
> . . . They got alarmed at the rapid progress of the
> gospel among the unclean Gentiles who threatened to
> soil the purity of the church. They could not close
> their eyes to the fact that the power was fast passing
> from Jerusalem to Antioch, and from the Jews to the
> Gentiles, but instead of yielding to the course of Provi-

dence, they determined to resist it in the name of order
and orthodoxy. . . . The agitation of these Judaizing
partisans and zealots brought the Christian church, twenty years after its founding, to the brink of a split which
would have seriously impeded its progress and endan-
gered its final success.*

It is hard for us to imagine how violent the con-
troversy was or how near the Church came to an
open split. "There was much disputing" and the
legalists tried to compel a test case of the circumcision of Titus. If the apostles had yielded for a
moment and the demand for circumcision had won
the day, Christianity as we know it would never
have survived. Christianity would have been rele-
gated to the status of a Jewish sect, and all who became members of the Church would first have been
Judaized and bound by the Law of Moses.

Peter at last stood up in strength and took over
the meeting for the apostles (15:7). He pointed out
that God had opened the door to the Gentiles
through his ministry and that the Gentiles, without
circumcision, had been led to a place of equality
and purity. Then Peter hit hard at circumcision itself, calling it a yoke that even the Jews had found
hard to bear (15:10, 11).

In the end grace triumphed over legalism, and
faith in Christ triumphed over ritual. Peter broke
the back of the opposition; Paul and Barnabas gave
testimony that delivered the final stroke (15:12);
and James, as apparent chairman of the council, ren-
dered the decision that buried the issue (15:13, 19,
20).

*Philip Schaff, History of the Christian Church, Vol. I, Apostolic
Christianity (Grand Rapids, Michigan: William B. Eerdmans, 1950),
pp. 338, 339.

The bonds of legalism were broken. This was a direct signal for a vigorous evangelization of the Gentiles. A letter admonishing the Gentile converts to continue in holiness was sent to the church in Antioch. When Paul and Barnabas returned to that city, (15:22-29), men named Judas and Silas went with them. When Judas returned finally to Jerusalem, Silas stayed on in Antioch. This was providential for God had a great work for him there.

C. PAUL AND BARNABAS SEPARATE
   (15:36-41)

With the theological crisis of the Church past, Paul suggested that he and Barnabas go again to Asia Minor and visit the churches they had established. Such a visit would encourage and strengthen the Galatian brethren. Barnabas, also eager for such a trip, wished to take John Mark with them. Paul, however, remembering the way Mark had deserted them in Pamphylia on the first trip, was determined that he should not go along. The two friends had such a sharp dispute that they decided not to make the trip together. There was a breach in their partnership, but not in their friendship.

Who was to blame? It is easy to place the blame on Barnabas for two reasons: Paul was the more outstanding and prominent man; and Mark was Barnabas' nephew. Some hold that this was a case of nepotism, with Barnabas favoring his nephew.

That is rather unfair to Barnabas. This man—whose name means "Son of Consolation"—was by nature a man of unusual forgiveness and patience. He had a genuine love for others. It was he who sold his property and gave the proceeds to the church; it was he who accepted Paul when many others were afraid and suspicious of him; it was he who sought Paul out and launched him into the work of God; he, furthermore, showed no resentment when Paul took the prominent place in their missionary partnership. It is likely that he would have been as kind and understanding to anyone else as he was to Mark.

Perhaps the treatment of both men served to make a man of Mark. The kind treatment of Barnabas would have encouraged the young man; the stern treatment of Paul very likely stiffened his fortitude and determination. It is good to know that later Mark became a strong man for God. Paul himself would commend him to the Colossians (Colossians 4:10) and would even send for him during his (Paul's) Roman imprisonment (2 Timothy 4:11). Twenty years later Paul would say of Mark: "He is profitable to me for the ministry." Peter referred to Mark as his son (1 Peter 5:13). And, perhaps, most significant of all was the fact that Mark would write one of the four Gospels on the life of Jesus. Such a man as this could not have been very bad, and Barnabas' kindness to him could not have been all wrong.

Perhaps it all worked for good. Now the Lord had two effective teams of missionaries. Barnabas and Mark sailed together to Cyprus. Paul chose Silas, a disciple recently come to Antioch from Jerusalem, to be his partner. They went through Syria, then by land to Cilicia in Asia Minor. This was Paul's homeland. There is no record how the churches were established there, but tradition relates that they were planted by Paul between the time of his conversion and his going to Antioch.

D. PAUL'S SECOND MISSIONARY JOURNEY (16:1—18:22)

1. Paul Finds Timothy in Lystra (16:1-5). From Cilicia Paul and Silas went to Derbe and Lystra, the furthermost cities reached on the first trip. It had been now about five years since that trip was made.

In Lystra Paul found that one of his converts on his earlier visit, a young man named Timothy, had blossomed into an outstanding Christian. Timothy was the son of a devout Jewess mother and a Greek father. His aged grandmother was also a woman of profound faith (2 Timothy 1:5), but evidently the father was a heathen.

Paul made Timothy a part of the missionary group. Then he circumcised him. After winning a victory over this matter so recently, one wonders why Paul now performed the controversial rite. Evidently it was because Timothy was half Jewish, and the decision in Jerusalem concerned Gentiles only.

Timothy proved to be a stalwart of the faith. He never flagged in his faithfulness either to Paul or to the Christian faith. Paul came to rely on Timothy more than anyone else and held him in such affection that he called him "my beloved son, and faithful in the Lord" (1 Corinthians 4:17).

Paul, Silas, and Timothy then visited the several churches in the region of Galatia and communicated to them the decrees and decisions set forth by the apostles and elders in Jerusalem.

2. The Macedonian Vision (16:6-10). As the group traveled westward across Asia Minor they were forbidden by the Holy Ghost to preach there. The doors were shut by the Spirit as they went from place to place. When Paul contemplated going north to Bithynia the Spirit said "No." When he considered preaching in any place of vast Asia Minor, the direction of the Spirit prohibited it.

It must have been a frustrating experience to feel such desire to preach, as Paul felt, and yet be restrained from doing so. But God had something else in mind for His apostle to the Gentiles. A broader field was immediately before him, a ministry unprecedented in prophetic or apostolic history. God was preparing him for labor in Europe.

In Troas, a seaport in the province of Mysia, on the westernmost border of Asia Minor, Paul had a vision. During the night, a man appeared in a vision to Paul and said, "Come over into Macedonia, and help us" (16:9). That was the answer to Paul's frustration about preaching in Asia. God had been preparing him for this new venture.

Macedonia was in Europe—the northern province of Greece famed in history as the home of Alexander the Great. Macedonia was rough, barbarian, and in great spiritual need. God wanted Paul in Macedonia, and His apostle did not hesitate to go.

Something notable happens here in the narrative of Acts. The account of the journey changes from the third person to the first: "*We* endeavoured to go" (16:10). This lets us know that Luke, the writer of Acts, joined the group in Troas. Luke was a Greek, perhaps even a Macedonian, who was apparently living in Troas. This physician and writer played an important part in the subsequent history of the Church.

3. Paul Goes to Philippi in Macedonia (16:11-40).
Paul and his associates—Silas, Timothy, and Luke—
sailed across the Aegean Sea to the port city of Ne-
apolis. Then they went into Philippi, the chief city
in that part of Macedonia. It was named for Philip,
warrior father of Alexander the Great who had uni-
fied and ruled Macedonia long ago. Now it was a
Roman colony, with a garrison of soldiers stationed
there to maintain Roman law and order. This necessarily gave Philippi a strong Roman influence. Paul,
being a Roman citizen, felt an understandable at-
traction to the city.

There was no synagogue in Philippi but the Jews
had a place of worship by a riverside just beyond
the city gate. Following his custom, Paul sought out
these Jews and preached first to them. Lydia, a
wealthy cloth merchant (purple cloth was very ex-
pensive), was converted and baptized along with her
household. This noble lady was the first European
convert to Christ. Following her conversion Lydia
insisted that Paul and his party stay at her house.

Paul met spiritual opposition in Philippi. A young
slave girl saw the missionary party and began to
follow Paul over the city saying, "These men are
the servants of the most high God, which shew unto
us the way of salvation." The girl had a spirit of
divination, which means that through evil spirits
she could foretell the future. Her owners made much
money by using her as a fortune-teller, though she
herself was given no more than food to eat and a
garment to wear. Paul was deeply moved with com-
passion for this pathetic young creature and cast
the evil spirit out of her.

Healed of her demon-possession, the girl could

no longer tell the future. This angered her owners, for their source of income was taken away. Instead of rejoicing that she was healed, these avaricious men had Paul and Silas arrested. They stirred up race hatred against the missionaries by calling attention to the fact that they were Jews (16:20). Paul and Silas were harshly treated. Without a trial, they were flogged, put into prison, and secured in stocks, or fetters.

During the night God took over for his mistreated servants as they prayed and sang with faith and spiritual joy. An earthquake so shook the prison that the doors flew open and the fetters were loosed. Before the night was over the jailer and his family were converted and baptized. This conversion immediately produced deeds of Christian charity; the jailer washed the prisoners' wounds and gave them food.

The next morning, the magistrates, who knew that there was no legal case against Paul and Silas, issued orders for their release. But the men of God were not interested in merely being set free, for God had already set them free during the night. The magistrates were to find that one could not so easily be rid of these men and their mission. Paul and Silas wanted the gospel vindicated and the dignity of the Christians restored. The scourging of Roman citizens was punishable by death, yet the magistrates had done this. Now, let them come to the prison in person and make public amends for the wrong they had done.

The magistrates were alarmed when they heard that the men they had so ill-regarded were Romans and men of influence. So they hastened to the prison

and made a public release of the innocent men. They
urged the missionaries to leave the city, probably
because of the anti-Semitic tumult that had been
stirred up.

Paul and his party took their leave of Philippi,
but they left behind them the seeds of an outstanding church. Luke evidently remained behind, for
the term *we* is discontinued here. It is believed that
Philippi was his home.

4. The Church in Thessalonica (17:1-9). Paul went
next to Thessalonica more than a hundred miles
south of Philippi. This was an important city, stra-
tegically located where the principal trade routes
of Macedonia intersected.

There were enough Jews in Thessalonica to maintain a synagogue. As was customary, Paul went to
this synagogue and preached. His message was usually the same: Jesus was crucified and buried; He rose
from the dead; He is the Christ, the Messiah.

During three straight Sabbaths of witnessing in
the synagogue, Paul won many of the Gentile worshipers to Christ. The Jews once again became en-
vious and stirred up trouble by inciting the rabble
of the city against Paul. These especially oppressed
Jason and his friends who were Christian converts
and probably kept the missionaries in their homes.
The mob falsely charged them with insurrection
against Caesar. Without intending to, they paid the
missionaries a high compliment by accusing them
before the magistrates of having "turned the world
upside down" (17:6).

Jason and His friends were not imprisoned but
were fined and enjoined to keep the peace (v. 9).

The result was that Paul and his companions left Thessalonica lest they bring further trouble to the new Christians. As in Philippi, however, they left a strong church in Thessalonica.

5. *In Berea (17:10-14)*. Paul preached next in Berea, about sixty miles west of Thessalonica. Here the Jews were of a higher sort then those in Thessalonica. They followed Paul's preaching intently and read the Scriptures to check his message with the Word of God.

Berea was one of the most favorable places Paul visited in Europe, yet it was, ironically, one of the few places where he apparently did not organize a church. Before he could complete his work, the Jews from Thessalonica came to Berea and stirred up hatred against him. Once again Paul had to flee for his life. The Berean brethren took him far south to the great city of Athens. Silas stayed in Berea, and Paul sent Timothy back to Thessalonica (1 Thessalonians 3:1, 2).

6. *Paul in Athens (17:15-34)*. When Paul went from Berea to Athens he went into a strikingly different world. Philippi, Thessalonica, and Berea were all in the northern Greek province of Macedonia, but Athens was in Achaia in the south. It was a city of culture, the most important metropolis in all Greece. It was the university center of the world, and men from all over the world were there seeking learning. Athens was also a city of religion—named for the goddess Athena. So many statues of the gods were in the city that they reportedly outnumbered those in all the rest of Greece. The Macedonian cities were provincial towns in comparison to Athens.

Paul was so disturbed by the prevalent idolatry that he pressed his witness of Christ in the Jewish synagogue and to the people in the marketplaces. It was inevitable that the philosophers would hear of him and ultimately meet him. They spent their time searching out and considering new truths and philosophies. Paul, preaching the crucifixion and resurrection of Jesus, quickly aroused their attention.

Two principal schools of Greek philosophy were Epicureanism and Stoicism. Simply stated, the Epicureans believed that wisdom causes a man to make the most of all pleasures available to him. Also simply stated, the Stoics believed that all human passions should be subjected to reason. The one taught the enjoyment of pleasure as an expression of wisdom; the other taught that virtue was best expressed in self-control.

Now they said, in the language of our day, "Let us hear what this crackpot has to say!"

The Athenian philosophers invited Paul to Areopagus, that is, Mars' Hill, a rocky knoll near the marketplace where orators delivered eloquent and judicial speeches. The most learned men of Greece spoke and sat in court on Mars' Hill. The Athenians were so pedantic that they would jeer and mock a man who mispronounced a single Greek syllable on Mars' Hill.

Paul bore witness to Christ in this honored place before some of the most learned men of his day. It was a masterful sermon in which he brought his own Greek learning into play. He brought to bear what he had seen in Athens (v. 23); he used his knowledge of Greek science (v. 26); he quoted Greek literature (v. 28); he built an irrefutable theological case for the nature of God; and he did it all in language so precise that none could gainsay him. When, however, he reached the point of his message, the resurrection of Jesus (v. 31), he ran into trouble.

The apostle was interrupted and could not complete his sermon. Some of the ruder listeners derided him and jeered him to silence. More polite listeners said, "We will hear thee again of this matter," which seems to have been only a courteous refusal to hear anything further from him.

A few Athenians did believe: Dionysius, one of the judges in the court of the Areopagus; a woman named Damaris; and a few others. Comparatively, nonetheless, Paul failed in Athens. He left the city abruptly, not because of persecution, or danger, or pressure from growing jealousy. He left with the sound of mockery and ridicule in his ears. He was not driven out, for Athens was too proud and sophisticated for such crude treatment as that—he was laughed out. "He quitted Athens and never returned to it," says Stalker. "Nowhere else had he failed so completely."

7. *The Church in Corinth (18:1-18)*. Still alone, Paul went to Corinth, about forty miles from Athens. As Athens was the cultural center of Greece, Corinth was its commercial center. It was located just south of the narrow isthmus where the sea almost cuts Greece in half. All traffic by land north and south, and all sea traffic from Europe to Asia, passed by Corinth. Its population was understandably a mixture from many lands. Vice was so prevalent in Corinth that "to Corinthianize" meant to lead a life of debauched, drunken abandonment. Of all

the cities Paul visited, Corinth seemed least promising for the gospel.

Here Paul formed a friendship with Aquila and Priscilla who were already Christians. He stayed in their home and worked with them weaving tent-cloth.

Paul attended the Corinthian synagogue and expounded the Scriptures to both Jews and Greeks. Remembering the results in Athens, he did not immediately preach Christ. Then Silas and Timothy arrived from Macedonia, and about the same time Paul was pressed in spirit to preach Christ. He did, and met instant hostility from the Jews.

The Jewish leaders were so hostile that Paul withdrew from the synagogue and, as he had done in Antioch of Pisidia, turned to the Gentiles. Christian worship was then started in the home of Justus, next door to the synagogue. Then the leader of the synagogue, Crispus, was converted. With this, the tension between the Jews and the Gentile Christians mounted until Paul was in grave danger. But God appeared to him and directed him to preach boldly, for no one would harm him (18:9, 10).

Paul did speak out. He remained in Corinth for a year and a half. More troubles came, such as the trial and riot at the judgment seat of Gallio (18:12-17), but a church was established. It was always Paul's problem church, as one might expect from the general background and character of the Corinthian people.

8. Back to Palestine (18:18-22). Paul left Europe when he left Corinth. He crossed the Aegean Sea to Asia Minor, on his way to Antioch and Jerusalem. Aquila and Priscilla went with him as far as Ephesus, where Paul taught in the synagogue. The response was favorable, and although the people desired him to remain with them, his urgent desire to attend the coming feast in Jerusalem (either the Passover or Pentecost) prevented his doing so. Aquila and Priscilla, however, remained in Ephesus. Then Paul continued to Palestine, with a promise to return to Ephesus if God willed it.

E. PAUL'S THIRD MISSIONARY JOURNEY (18:23—20:5)

1. Passage Through Galatia (18:23). Paul's third missionary journey was largely one in which he consolidated the gains of his first two. He departed from Antioch and traveled across the vast landmass of Asia Minor toward Ephesus, on the extreme western Asian coast. Before reaching Ephesus the apostle passed through the sprawling province of Galatia.

Though it is summed up in one verse (18:23), Paul's time in Galatia was important to the churches he had established on his first journey. The congregations in Lystra, Iconium, and Antioch in the district of Pisidia on the border of Phrygia, were strengthened by his visit among them.

Paul went from the country of Galatia to Ephesus, where he stayed for three years. This was the real objective of his third journey, so most of his labors were there, and most of this section of Acts concerns the Ephesian ministry.

2. Apollos' Ministry in Ephesus (18:24-28). Apollos was a Jewish Christian from Alexandria, Egypt. He was eloquent, deep in the Scriptures, very zealous, and instructed in the way of the Lord. These qualifications made him a diligent teacher in the synagogue at Ephesus where he taught effectively the things of Christ.

Apollos, however, had one deficiency: His knowledge of the way of God was incomplete. He had possibly been to Judea during the days of Jesus and had heard the message of repentance unto salvation. This he believed and accepted with all his heart, and this he preached with contagious conviction. He believed that Jesus was the promised Messiah, and seems to have won many converts to the way of the Lord.

After Aquila and Priscilla heard Apollos preach, they apparently took him to their home and gave him further instruction in the way of the Lord. Exactly what this means is seen in 19:2-6. Apollos was led into a depth of spiritual enlightenment and experience that is possible only through the Passion of Christ and the infusion of the Holy Ghost. There is no indication that Apollos' knowledge of Jesus was erroneous, only incomplete. He needed that deeper, "more perfect," knowledge of the coming of the Holy Spirit in power.

The impression is strong that the effectiveness of Apollos increased when he was led into this deeper understanding. He went from Ephesus to Achaia in Greece (18:27), where he preached with outstanding results in Corinth (1 Corinthians 1:12). He became so popular that an Apollos faction was formed within the Corinthian church.

3. *The Ephesians Receive the Holy Spirit (19:1-10).* When Paul passed through Ephesus on his earlier journey, he promised to return (18:20, 21). At last

he fulfilled that promise. After his visit with the Galatian churches, he made his way to the bustling city of Ephesus, capital of the Roman province of Asia. The apostle stayed in the wicked, worldly, idolatrous city for nearly three years, and most of Acts 19 is concerned with his ministry there.

In Ephesus Paul found a group of twelve disciples who, like Apollos, had incomplete understanding of the Christian experience. It is not likely, however, that these disciples (and the word "certain" indicates that this was a particular group) were acquainted with either Apollos or Aquila and Priscilla. If they had been they would have heard about the Holy Ghost.

These twelve men were Christians, as is strongly affirmed by the use of the words "disciples" and "believed."

That these men were Christians is certainly to be inferred from the way in which Luke describes them as "disciples"; this is a term which he commonly uses for Christians, and had he meant to indicate that they were disciples not of Christ but of John the Baptist (as has sometimes been deduced from v. 3), he would have said so explicitly. . . . At any rate, Paul's question, "Did ye receive the Holy Spirit when ye believed?" suggests strongly that he regarded them as true believers in Christ.*

The reply of these disciples was that they had not even heard of the Holy Ghost. It is impossible that they could have meant that they had not heard of the person, the dispensation or office work of the Holy Spirit. What they obviously meant was that

*F. F. Bruce, *Commentary on the Book of the Acts* (*The New International Commentary*, edited by Ned B. Stonehouse. Grand Rapids, Michigan: William B. Eerdmans Publishing Company, 1954), p. 385.

they did not know that this deepening, enriching, empowering experience was available to all who had believed unto salvation.

So Paul baptized the disciples and laid his hands upon them. The Holy Ghost came on them and they spoke with tongues and prophesied.

4. Paul's Great Works (19:8-12). For three months Paul preached in the Ephesian synagogue, as he had done in so many other places. The results were also similar. Opposition arose until he was forced to find other worship quarters. Tyrannus, who operated a school in the city, offered his facilities to the Christians. In one old account of this period it is recorded that Paul used the school from 11 a.m. to 4 p.m. each day. Tyrannus held his classes in the early morning.

During his long ministry in Ephesus Paul's influence spread throughout Asia so that great and special works were done by the Lord through him. Luke tells us that these special miracles were wrought through the agency of handkerchiefs or aprons that had come into contact with his body. This is similar to the manner in which Peter's shadow had wrought healings in Jerusalem (5:16).

It is likely that the other six churches of Asia mentioned in Revelation (Revelation 1:11) were founded during this two-year period. These churches were started by Paul's fellow laborers, who apparently went out from Ephesus to other cities. Colosse was another Asian city reached with the gospel about this time. So it was that through Paul's influence "all they which dwelt in Asia heard the word of the Lord Jesus, both Jews and Greeks (19:10)."

5. The Sons of Sceva (19:13-20). One of the most

unusual incidents of the book of Acts is recorded here. Seven brothers, the sons of a Jew named Sceva, were itinerant Gypsy-like religious charlatans. They were exorcists, which means that they were professional healers who made the supposed casting-out-of-devils their trade. By preying on the superstitious people of Asia they no doubt became successful imposters. Through the use of various impressive-sounding formulas they convinced the afflicted and demon-possessed persons that they had worked a genuine spell or charm.

Observing Paul's miraculous works, these men tragically assumed that he was of the same trade and trickery as they. They added the name of Jesus, which Paul used in his prayers for the sick, to their list of incantations. Then they spoke this new charm on those they pretended to heal. They even added the name of Paul to their ritual: "We adjure you by Jesus whom Paul preaches!"

Then the charlatans made a near-fatal error. They rashly attempted to drive a real demon out. The demon resisted and the possessed man very nearly killed all seven of the men.

One can play at religion only so long. When the real forces of evil are met, one should be sure that he has the real Spirit in his own heart. When the Ephesians saw the folly and danger of magic and superstition they feared God greatly. They built a bonfire and burned more than ten thousand dollars' worth of books on magic and witchcraft as they turned from their superstition.

6. *The Riot in Ephesus (19:21-41)*. The incident recorded here is so full and complete that it admits

of little further comment or observation.

It happened that a riot broke out in Ephesus at a time when Paul was preparing for a trip into Macedonia and Achaia (19:21, 22). He sent Timothy and Erastus to Macedonia before him, but before he could leave, a silversmith named Demetrius incited his fellow craftsmen to riot. The provocation was Paul's preaching against idols, for this seemed to be cutting into the sales of the silver images of Diana.

In the mythology of the ancient world Diana was the goddess of fertility, represented as having many breasts for the nourishment of the earth. She was said to have descended from Jupiter, king of the gods (19:35). Diana was one of the chief deities of Asia. A temple had been built in Ephesus of such splendor that it was classed as one of the seven wonders of the world.

Using the rallying cry "Great is Diana of the Ephesians!" the silversmiths whipped the whole city into an uproar. The throng abducted two of Paul's companions, Gaius and Aristarchus, and rushed them into the city's open-air theater. The huge ten-thousand-seat amphitheater became the scene of utter confusion. A Jew named Alexander tried to stanch the emotional madness of the people but the mob screamed all the more. For two hours the people chanted their praise to Diana, few knowing what the tumult was all about. When Paul was persuaded not to go in after his friends, as he desired to do, and as the abductors probably hoped he would, the uproar gradually wore itself out. One of the city officials took over and explained that Paul and his friends had not criticized Diana by name and had not robbed her temples. Moreover, if Demetrius had

a complaint against the Christians they could settle
it in a legal and orderly manner. Then the official
dismissed the emotionally-exhausted assembly.

7. Paul's Return to Europe (20:1-5). After about
three years Paul left Ephesus. He went to Macedonia,
where he preached again in Philippi and Thessalonica. Then he went down to Corinth in Achaia
where he remained for three months. When he was
ready to leave Greece, he received word of a plot
against his life, changed his course, and retraced his
steps through Macedonia.

Thus Paul began his long third journey by visiting those churches he had founded in Galatia on
his first journey and concluded it with a visit to
the Greek churches he founded on his second journey.

F. PAUL'S FINAL JOURNEY TO JERUSALEM
   (20:6—21:17)

Luke presents a rather detailed account of Paul's
long journey back to Jerusalem. Most of Acts 20
and much of Acts 21 concerns this eventful voyage.
The apostle made several stops along the way—in
Troas (20:6-12); in Miletus (20:13-38); in Tyre
(21:1-6); and in Caesarea (21:7-14). In each of these
places he had a significant experience.

In studying this interesting section of Acts we
should bear in mind that Paul was now at least sixty
years of age. For twenty of those years he had been
in the service of his Saviour and his body was now
weary from unbroken, almost unbelievable, toils and
hardships. He had been away from Palestine for
three years and his longing to return is clearly seen.

1. In Troas (20:6-12), on the Asian shores of the Aegean Sea, Paul spent about a week with the Christians of that city. On his final night in Troas he preached an extremely long sermon. Adam Clarke supposes that he must have preached at least six hours. The meeting was on the third floor, and the room was filled with blazing lights. These oil lamps made the room exceptionally stuffy, so that a young man named Eutychus went to sleep and fell to the ground from the window where he was sitting.

Eutychus seems to have been killed by the fall—though the language of Paul in verse 10 does not clearly affirm that view. At any rate, Paul revived the young man and the people rejoiced to see him alive. The meeting continued through the remainder of the night, with the apostle in earnest discussion and conversation with his friends. What a happy occasion of fellowship that all-night service must have been!

2. In Miletus (20:13-38), a southern seaport of Asia, Paul sent to Ephesus for the elders of the church to come to him. Because he desired desperately to be in Jerusalem for the Feast of Pentecost he did not want to be away from the ship when favorable winds arose. So he sent word for the elders to make the three-day journey to him.

Paul's visit with the elders is one of the most touching scenes in the Bible. The aging apostle reviewed with them how he had worked among them "with many tears" and "from house to house." Paul warned the brethren of dangers ahead for them and commended them to God and to the Word of His grace.

The apostle pointed out four times that he had withheld nothing from the Ephesians (vv. 20, 27, 31, 35); and twice he mentioned how he had wept among them (vv. 19, 31).

The apostle saw the danger that awaited him in Jerusalem and knew that he was with his Ephesian friends for the last time. The elders, grieved in heart, wept and prayed with Paul before departing. Paul, knowing the danger but bound in his spirit to go on, continued his journey to Jerusalem.

3. In Tyre (21:1-5), as he neared Judea, Paul was specifically warned not to go to Jerusalem. During the week he spent with the Tyrian Christians, the Spirit gave voice to the danger that awaited him. But the apostle went on.

4. In Caesarea (21:6-14), Paul stayed in the home of Philip, who had led the Samaritan revival many years before. While there, a prophet named Agabus bound himself with Paul's girdle to show that the Jews would bind the apostle and turn him over to the Romans for judgment.

When the Caesarean Christians heard this they, and Paul's companions, as had the Ephesians and Tyrians, urged him not to go to Jerusalem. But some imperative urging, known only to him, drove him onward.

Then Paul answered, What mean ye to weep and to break mine heart? for I am ready not to be bound only, but also to die at Jerusalem for the name of the Lord Jesus (Acts 21:13).

5. In Jerusalem (21:15-17). At long last the journey was over. Paul and his companions, who reconciled

themselves to the apostle's determination, reached
Jerusalem in time for the celebration of Pentecost.
It was a solemn company that entered the Holy City
that day. Certainly the morbid reputation of the
sacred site—"killer of the prophets"—was on the
minds of many as they saw it gleaming in the sun
before them.

Imprisonment of Paul

Acts 21:18—28:31

A. PAUL ARRESTED IN JERUSALEM
(21:18—23:22)

The prophecy of Agabus was not long in coming to pass. Paul was arrested before he had been in Jerusalem a week.

The apostle was received with joy by James, the brother of Jesus, and by the other Christian leaders. The report of his work among the Gentiles caused much rejoicing. The elders, however, knew what resentment existed over Paul's de-emphasis of the Mosaic Law. This, even to thousands of Christian Jews, was a Law that must be kept. As a means of proving his faithfulness as a Jew, Paul was persuaded to take a Jewish vow (21:23, 24). This was not difficult for him, for Paul had previously taken such a vow (18:18); he had circumcised Timothy (16:3); he attended the Jewish feasts (18:21); and he always went first to the synagogue in every city. Nevertheless, the apostle took the advice of his elders in the Lord. This is to his great credit. He was a leader of men, yet he willingly accepted the authority of other men. Before a man is qualified to give orders

111

he must be willing to follow orders.

In the course of their ceremonial purification, Paul and the four fellow Christians who had taken the vow went into the Temple to make their sacrifice (21:26). There Paul was spotted by a group of non-Christian Jews from Ephesus. These men raised a cry against the apostle that alarmed all those in the Temple area. A rumor that Paul had brought a Greek into the Temple spread quickly, and the rumor ignited a riot.

Before the Jews could kill Paul, Roman soldiers from the fortress Antonia, adjacent to the Temple, heard of the tumult and rushed into the mob. The Romans arrested Paul and bound him with chains but could not make sense of the confused charges the Jews brought against him. The soldiers actually carried Paul bodily lest the violent mass of people kill him.

After calmly communicating his identity to the Roman captain, Paul was allowed to defend himself with a speech to the mob. He gave a long rehearsal of his life (22:1-21), but the people even more madly demanded his death.

Paul then had to rely on his Roman citizenship to get a fair hearing. When the Roman officer learned of Paul's status (22:25-30), he saw to it that the accused man had a chance to defend himself. Roman law could be hard, but it was fair-minded. From here on, Paul's Roman rights would stand between him and death.

The Sanhedrin was called together for an official hearing on the following day. During Paul's defense of himself to the Sanhedrin he displayed one understandable flare of indignation that happily reminds us that he was a man of such passions as we are. When the high priest had him slapped, the badgered apostle retorted: "God shall smite thee, thou whited wall: for sittest thou to judge me after the law, and commandest me to be smitten contrary to the law?" (Acts 23:3).

His words were full of bitter truth and scathing sarcasm toward the pious law-breaking of one who was supposed to be dispensing law. Another burst of passion from Paul shows what duress he was under. He made a strong, emotional appeal to the Pharisees of the council, observing to them his own Pharisaical background (23:6). This was a deliberate appeal to them for justice, which he realized he could not get from either the high priest or the Sadducees on the council. His overt appeal to factionalism resulted in a disordered tumult which left the meeting divided between the Pharisees and Sadducees. Paul gained support but not victory.

Because of the tumult, the Romans had to keep Paul in custody. The priests hated this one they regarded as a betrayer too much to see or hear him dispassionately. The orthodox Jews hated him so violently that a band of forty men took an oath to kill him (23:12-22).

God stood with His servant. "Be of good cheer, Paul," He said, "for as thou hast testified of me in Jerusalem, so must thou bear witness also at Rome" (23:11). Hereafter, everything that happened was just another step toward the Imperial City.

B. IMPRISONMENT AT CAESAREA
   (23:23—26:32)

1. Paul's Defense Before Felix (23:23—24:27). Because of the threat on Paul's life, the Roman captain, named Claudius Lysias, sent him to the Roman
stronghold in Caesarea. He addressed a letter explaining the case to Felix, the new procurator of
Judea. Two hundred soldiers, two hundred spear-
men, and seventy horsemen were dispatched to guard
the chained apostle on the journey, which was begun
during the night.

Felix waited five days for the trial in order that
Paul's accusers might have time to reach Caesarea.
The Jewish prosecutor, an orator named Tertullus,
opened the case by flattering the procurator (24:2,
3), and then gave the charges against Paul (vv. 5-7).
The charges ranged from silly grievances ("this fellow is a pest") to outright lies ("a mover of sedition,"
and "who hath also gone about to profane the Temple"). Tertullus also tried to make it appear that
Paul would have been arrested in an orderly way
by the Jews except for the interference of Lysius—
which was another lie.

Paul's defense of himself was an orderly refutation
of these charges. This one speech, as much as any
other, shows the methodical processes of his great
mind and his knowledge of law, both Roman and
Jewish. First, he demonstrated that he was not an
insurrectionist: he had no mob with him in Jerusalem; he engaged in no debates in the Temple,
the synagogues, nor in the city. How, then, could
he be accused of sedition?

Then he showed how conscientiously he had worshiped God. The hope of the resurrection was his
driving force and anchoring faith. The greatest ob-
jection the Jews had to him was his faith in the

Resurrection—for the Jews themselves were divided on this doctrine. Moreover, they were angered because Paul's faith was based upon the resurrection of Jesus.

In his defense Paul also mentioned that he had brought alms to his people. This may give us the reason for his determination to go to Jerusalem despite all the warnings against it. Throughout his third journey he had been raising funds for relief of the disciples in Judea. It is possible that he felt he must deliver this store in person.

As a lawyer, Tertullus was no match for Paul. One by one the apostle put the charges down. Furthermore, as he pointed out, the real accusers, the Ephesian Jews, had not even come to face him.

Felix was both shrewd and discerning. He saw that there was no real case against Paul. To condemn him would be unjust, and to acquit him would arouse the Jews' ill will toward his administration. Felix was also upset by the words of Paul; trembling, he indicated his desire to hear more about the gospel of Christ when he could consider it thoroughly (24:24). He was also greedy, for he hoped that Paul might offer a bribe for his release (24:26).

Paul refused to do this, so Felix refused to take action on the case. The apostle was therefore kept in prison for two years.

2. *Paul's Defense Before Festus (25:1-12).* When Paul had been in the Caesarean prison for two years, Festus succeeded Felix as procurator of Judea. But during all this time the hatred of the priests had not abated. They requested that Paul be sent to Jerusalem for trial, hoping the new governor would

grant the wishes of so influential a body. They never expected the apostle to reach Jerusalem, however, for he would be murdered along the way.

Festus refused. Paul must be tried by Roman law in Caesarea. Note the eagerness of the priests: they made their original request of Festus only three days after his arrival in Jerusalem; and they arrived in Caesarea ready for the trial the day following Festus' arrival in that city (25:1, 6, 7).

The trial before Festus is briefly reported, which indicates that it must have followed the general lines of the trial before Felix. The new procurator did endeavor, however, to please the priests. He asked Paul if he were prepared to go to Jerusalem and stand trial there. This was an overt concession to Jewish influence. After all, Festus reasoned, he must have the favor of the Jewish leaders if he were going to succeed as procurator. And he did want to succeed.

Paul's reaction was immediate. He must have thought much about this eventuality during the two years in prison. His well-thought-out reply was destined to change the course of his trial and influence the course of the Church. Paul knew that he was being used as a pawn to curry the favor of his powerful enemy. But the apostle had one great advantage as a Roman citizen: he could appeal his case to the Caesar in Rome. So he said,

"I am standing in Caesars court and that is where I should be judged. I have done the Jews no harm, as you very well know. It comes to this: if I were a criminal and had committed some crime which deserved the death penalty, I should not try to evade sentence of death. But as in fact there is no truth in the accusations these men have made, I am not

prepared to be used as a means of gaining their favor—
I *appeal to Caesar!*" (Acts 25:10, 11, *Phillips Translation*).*

Once Paul made this decision there was no turning back. Reluctant as he may have been to make
the appeal, which was the ultimate assertion of al-
legiance to Rome, Paul had no other choice. He
may have interpreted the vision of Jesus as instruct-
ing him to do so when He said, "Thou must bear
witness also at Rome" (23:11).

Whatever his reasons were, Paul made good and
wise use of the advantage his citizenship provided
him. Festus was deeply upset by this unexpected
stroke by the insignificant-appearing little man before him. His very first case as procurator was ap-
pealed from his court to that of Caesar's. After con-
sultation with his council, he did all he could do:
he granted the appeal.

3. Paul's Defense Before Agrippa (25:13—26:32).
Agrippa II, son of the Agrippa of Acts 12:20-23,
came to Caesarea for a state visit. The Bernice who
accompanied Agrippa was his sister, not his wife.
Festus told the king about the presence of Paul in
his prison, awaiting transfer to Rome for trial. Festus
was in quite a dilemma, for he did not know what
to write Caesar Augustus concerning the difficult
case (25:26). The Jews insisted that the prisoner be
put to death, but it was obvious he had done nothing
worthy of death. There was no question of broken
laws or rebellion—only matters of Jewish theology.
The real grievance against Paul was his preaching
that Jesus had been raised from the dead and was
yet alive (25:19).

Op. cit.

Agrippa, who had evidently heard of Paul, desired to see him and hear what he had to say. A hearing was arranged for the next day for the king and several prominent townsmen.

Virtually all of Acts 26 is a record of Paul's defense before Agrippa. Here he made what was probably his greatest speech. It has been called his formal declaration of the Christian life. In the unaccustomed atmosphere of calm consideration he reviewed his background as a Jew, a Pharisee, a persecutor of the name of Christ, and at last a convert to the Christian faith. He dwelt at length on the vision Christ gave him at his conversion (26:13-19), a vision that had been the impulse of his life and labors. It was for these labors that the Jews had determined to kill him—not because of any wrong he had done (vv. 20, 21). And his labors had centered in the hope of Israel and the promise of the fathers (vv. 6, 7), which hope was fulfilled in the resurrection of Jesus Christ (vv. 8, 22, 23).

The message of the Resurrection had its usual effect on unbelievers. Festus the Roman procurator concluded that Paul was mad with much learning; Agrippa, the Judean king, admitted that with a little persuasion Paul would have made him a Christian (v. 28). Whether this was said in sincerity or sarcasm makes little difference, for nothing was changed at all. The king remained vile; the governor remained weak; and Paul remained in bonds.

C. THE VOYAGE TO ROME (27:1—28:31)

1. The Storm and Shipwreck (27:1-44). The final two chapters of Acts record Paul's voyage to Rome.

The story is told vividly and with great detail. Luke uses the first person in the narrative, which indicates that he was aboard the ship with Paul. The purpose of the long account is to show how God stood by His servant in the bleakest hour of his life, and how this man of God was, even as a prisoner in chains, the master of all about him.

Paul, along with other prisoners being sent to Rome, was put aboard a ship bound for ports of Asia Minor. Julius, centurion of the guard, let Paul go freely over the ship and visit with his friends, Aristarchus and Luke, who were permitted to accompany the apostle. Luke gave exact details of the ship's movements as the voyage progressed to and through the storm and shipwreck. It was a long voyage against adverse winds, with a change of ships at Myra, on the coast of Asia Minor. The ship then labored south-westward, tacking against eastward winds, so that it moved slowly along the southern coast of Crete. Winter was approaching and further sailing had become dangerous.

Paul warned that he foresaw hurt and damage ahead if they went on beyond Fair Havens. The owner and captain disagreed, so they sailed on, hoping to spend the winter in Phenice on the south-western end of Crete. After all, what would an itinerant Jewish preacher know about ships and gales?

The ship never reached Phenice, for it soon ran into a storm of great intensity. The crew could not control the direction of the ship, so they let it drive before the wind. They fought day and night against the storm. Then Paul, after a period of fasting, had a vision in which the Lord assured him that no life would be lost (27:21-25).

It was as Paul said. After fourteen days and nights
of the storm, the ship approached unknown land.
The men cast out their anchors lest they be dashed
on the rocks in the night. When day came the ship
was wrecked against the shore but all 276 persons
aboard the ship were saved.

The story of the storm and shipwreck is one of
the most detailed and exciting adventures recorded
anywhere in Holy Writ. It deserves careful reading
because of its spiritual lessons. The course of the
storm brought Paul to the depth of his human experience, but God then undertook when all hope
was gone and lifted him to a new pinnacle of influence and power. The ship would have sunk had not
Paul been aboard, but because of him 275 others
were spared from death.

2. *On Melita (28:1-10)*. The ship had wrecked on
Melita, a small island south of Italy. The natives
were barbarians, a term given to any people who
did not speak Greek, which by no means inferred
that they were savages. Melita was a colony of Phoenicia and Carthage at that time; today it is known
as Malta.

A viper bit Paul as he was putting wood on a fire
that had been built for the comfort of the weary,
drenched men of the ship. Seeing this, the islanders
took Paul to be a murderer fleeing justice. When the
snakebite had no ill effect on him, their superstitious
minds went to the other extreme and they thought
surely he must be a god (28:3-6).

Paul's immunity to the snake's venom was a fulfillment of Christ's promise in Luke 10:19, when

He sent the seventy disciples out, and in Mark 16:18, when He gave His great commission to the disciples. This is the only incident of such a miracle in the New Testament, yet it serves to exemplify the purpose of Christ's promise.

Paul did another notable miracle on Melita. The chief man of the island, whose name was Publius, owned an estate near where the ship wrecked. The group of passengers stayed on his estate for three days, during which Paul healed Publius' father of dysentery (v. 8). When the citizens of Melita heard of this, many afflicted persons came to the apostle for healing.

The large group remained on the island for three months, during which time they were all treated hospitably. When favorable sailing weather returned with early spring, the group set sail in an Alexandrian grain ship which also had wintered on Crete. The name of the ship was Castor and Pollux, or Twin Brothers, so named for the mythological gods of seafaring men.

3. Paul Arrives in Rome (28:11-16). The voyage on to Rome went smoothly. With landings at Syracuse on the large island of Sicily, and Rhegium on the toe of Italy, the ship sailed to Puteoli on the Italian coast near the Bay of Naples. This port also served Rome, though the Imperial City was a considerable distance to the north.

Paul and his companions, Luke and Aristarchus, found Christian brethren in Puteoli. Somehow they managed to visit a full week with these disciples before continuing their journey. Word went ahead that the apostle was on his way to Rome, so delega-

tions of Christians from Rome met Paul in Apaii
Forum and Three Taverns, small towns about thirty
miles south of Rome. The aged apostle was greatly
encouraged by the greeting from these brethren.
They marched along with the apostle into the great
city. Though he was a prisoner, they made his entry
an occasion of gladness and triumph. There was no
sadness or defeat for either the gospel or its great
apostle that day.

Paul was properly handled as a prisoner in Rome,
yet with deference and respect. He was not put in
a prison but was allowed to secure his own quarters,
where a guard kept him in technical custody.

4. Paul's Prison Ministry (28:17-31). In Rome Paul
followed his custom of communicating first with
Jews and then with the Gentiles. Inasmuch as he
could not go to them, he invited the leading Jews
of the city to visit him and explained why he was a
prisoner. The Jews had not heard of his journey or
even of his arrest in Jerusalem. But they had heard
about the Christian sect—and all they had heard was
bad (28:22). Still, the Jews wished to hear what the
apostle had to say. In their eyes he was still a Jew,
a rabbi, a Pharisee. None of these identities could
be taken from him. And he so regarded himself—
holding that he was a Messianic Jew, a prisoner because of the hope of Israel (v. 20).

The Jews returned later with a larger delegation
to hear and consider this Christian message of Paul.
He earnestly endeavored to show these leaders that
the Kingdom of God had arrived; it had not come
with geographic dimensions, but with the advent
of Jesus of Nazareth, who was the hope of Israel and

the fulfillment of the Law and the prophets (28:23).

The usual pattern prevailed: Some in the audience were persuaded by the gospel; others rejected it. Paul was grieved by the rejection and asked to say one last word. Quoting Isaiah 6:9, 10 to show how, in their dullness of heart, God's people had refused to understand, Paul declared that the gospel of salvation thenceforth would go to the Gentiles. This was the final sharp line between Jew and Christian. Hereafter they would grow increasingly farther apart.

For two years Paul remained in legal custody in his own house. He was not kept from his work but was permitted to preach freely to all who came to him (28:30, 31). Not only did he preach in this way, but he also wrote letters of doctrine and exhortation to distant places where he had been. Philippians, Colossians, Ephesians, and Philemon were almost certainly written during these two years.

Evidently Luke wrote the book of Acts during this period of imprisonment, for here the narrative ends. We can turn to other sources and learn how the matter turned out, but when Luke wrote the Book of Acts he did not know. So it is best for us to leave it there.

And although the Book of Acts closes with its greatest exponent imprisoned, the gospel for which he stood went forth, and still goes forth, liberating the hearts of men.

REVIEW AND DISCUSSION

1. How does Acts set a pattern for our day?
2. Why is Acts of the Apostles not a completely accurate designation for the book? Suggest additional names for the book.
3. Who wrote the book of Acts? What proof do you have of his authorship?
4. DISCUSS: the various ways one could outline the Book of Acts.
5. What is the meaning of the word "pentecost"?
6. What is the significance and meaning of "with one accord" in Acts?
7. What is meant by the first witnesses (Acts 2:5-13)?
8. DISCUSS: the different results of Peter's sermons in Acts 2 and Acts 4.
9. Who was Nicholas?
10. DISCUSS: Saul's persecution of the early Christians.
11. What significance was the church of Antioch to the spread of the Christian faith?
12. How did the death of Herod affect the early church?
13. How did Gamaliel contribute to the progress of the early church?
14. Why is Chapter 15 one of the most important sections of Acts?
15. TRACE: Paul's First Missionary Journey.
16. Why was Paul stoned at Lystra?
17. DISCUSS: Paul and Barnabas's separation. What were the results?
18. TRACE: Paul's Second Missionary Journey.
19. Exactly what happened on Mar's Hill?
20. TRACE: Paul's Third Missionary Journey.
21. What happened in Acts 19?
22. Describe Paul's final journey to Jerusalem.
23. DISCUSS: Paul's defense before Felix, Festus, and Agrippa.
24. What happened on Paul's voyage to Rome?
25. DISCUSS: Paul's prison ministry.

ANNOTATED BOOK LIST

Good books on Acts of the Apostles are abundant. The student of Acts will do well to make use of this wealth of material. In this bibliography I have listed those which I have found to be of particular benefit. Some are for elementary study while others are for the advanced student.

Alexander, Joseph Addison, *Commentary on the Acts of the Apostles*. Grand Rapids, Michigan: Zondervan Publishing House, 1956. This old classic, in an attractive new edition, is very helpful and thorough in treatment.

Barclay, William, *The Acts of the Apostles*, Vol. VII of *Daily Study Bible Series*. Philadelphia: The Westminster Press, 1955. Barclay has produced one of the finest devotional commentaries to appear in recent years. This is of great value.

Blaiklock, E. M., *The Acts of the Apostles*, Vol. V of *Tyndale New Testament Commentaries*, ed. R.V.G. Tasker. Grand Rapids, Michigan: William B. Eerdmans Publishing Company, 1959. This volume is a simple, yet profound, treatment of the Acts.

Bruce, F. F., *Commentary on the Book of the Acts*, Vol. V of *The New International Commentary on the New Testament*, ed. Ned B. Stonehouse. Grand Rapids, Michigan: William B. Eerdmans Publishing Company, 1954. In many ways this is one of the finest books available. Though it is the work of a scholar, and is for scholars, it is simple enough for the average student. I also call your attention to Bruce's *The Acts of the Apostles: Commentary on the Greek Text*. Its excellence will be especially appreciated by the advanced student.

Carter, Charles W. and Earle Ralph, *The Acts of the Apostles*, Vol. II of *The Evangelical Commentary*, et al. ed. George Allen Turner. Grand Rapids, Michigan: Zondervan Publishing House, 1959. Warmly recommended for its evangelical treatment of Acts. Of particular value to the holiness reader.

Erdman, Charles R., *The Acts*, Vol. V of *Expositions on the*

New Testament. Philadelphia: Westminster Press, 1919. This little volume never fails to provide inspiration and assistance of great volume.

Gaebelein, Arno C., *The Acts of the Apostles, An Exposition.* New York: Loizeaux Brothers, 1961. A deeply spiritual study of Acts. Of tremendous value to the evangelical student.

Griffith-Thomas, W. H., *Outline Studies in the Acts of the Apostles,* Grand Rapids, Michigan: William B. Eerdmans Publishing Company, 1956. Warmly evangelical outline and analysis, with notes and comments.

Hackett, Horatio B., *A Commentary on the Acts of the Apostles,* Vol. IV of *An American Commentary on the New Testament,* ed. Alvah Hovey. Philadelphia: The American Baptist Publication Society, 1882. An older work of solid scholarship.

Keck, Leander E., *Mandate to Witness.* Chicago: The Judson Press, 1964. A newly published study of the witnessing aspects of Acts.

Maclaren, Alexander, *The Acts of the Apostles, Maclaren's Bible Class Exposition.* Grand Rapids, Michigan: Zondervan Publishing House, 1959. Excellent studies by a master expositor.

Moorehead, William G., *Outline Studies in the New Testament: Acts to Ephesians.* Grand Rapids, Michigan: Baker Book House, 1953. Contains a generous treatment of the Book of Acts.

Morgan, G. Campbell, *The Acts of the Apostles.* New York: Fleming H. Revell Company, 1924. One of the outstanding expositions on Acts in the English language.

Phillips, J. B., *The Young Church in Action.* New York: The Macmillan Company, 1955. This translation of Acts is the best modern English version available. Reading it is like reading the Acts of the Apostles for the first time. The translation of Acts is also included in the complete New Testament translation, *The New Testa-*

ment in Modern English by J. B. Phillips, The Macmillan Company, 1958.

Purves, George T., *Christianity in the Apostolic Age*. Grand Rapids, Michigan: Baker Book House, 1955. A classic study of undiminished value and interest.

Rackman, R. B., *The Acts of the Apostles*. Grand Rapids, Michigan: Baker Book House, 1964. One of the most outstanding books ever published on Acts, in a beautiful new edition. Definitely a scholar's work.

Robertson, A. T., *Studies in the New Testament*. Nashville, Tennessee: Broadman Press, 1949. An elementary treatment for the young or beginning student.

Robertson, A. T., *The Acts of the Apostles,* Vol. III of *Word Pictures in the New Testament*. New York: Harper & Brothers, 1930. This is based on the Greek text. A scholarly work unsurpassed for analytical value.

Schaff, Phillip, *Apostolic Christianity,* Vol. I of *History of the Christian Church*. Grand Rapids, Michigan: William B. Eerdmans, 1950. This first volume of Dr. Schaff's massive history of Christianity deals with those events covered by Acts. It is massive, scholarly, and rich.

Stagg, Frank, *The Book of Acts*. Nashville, Tennessee: Broadman Press, 1955. One of the finest books on Acts to appear in our generation. This has the markings of a classic study.

Thomas, David, *Acts of the Apostles*. Grand Rapids, Michigan: Baker Book House, 1955. An extensive older treatment of Acts in a pleasant new edition.

Williams, R. R., *The Acts of the Apostles,* Vol. V of *Torch Bible Commentaries,* et al., ed. John Marsh. London: S.C.M. Press, 1953. A short and pithy commentary of scholarly proportions, but with liberal leanings.

Winn, Albert C., *The Acts of the Apostles,* Vol. XX of *The Layman's Bible Commentary,* ed. Balmer H. Kelley. Richmond, Virginia: John Knox Press, 1960. This is especially helpful but has a definite liberal slant.